Soggy Shrub Rides Again,

and other improbabilities

Soggy Shrub
Rides Again,
and other improbabilities
by James Smart

Foreword by Clark DeLeon
Illustrated by Bea Weidner

Enoch Flower

Blue Flower

Philadelphia 1995

Soggy Shrub Rides Again, and other improbabilities
by James Smart

Illustrated by Bea Weidner

Designed by Barbara Torode

Enoch Flower Publishing, P. O. Box 27666
Philadelphia PA 19118.

Library of Congress Cataloging-in-Publication Data

Smart, James, 1930 Apr. 27-
Soggy Shrub Rides Again and other improbabilities / James Smart ;
foreword by Clark DeLeon ; illustrated by Bea Weidner. — 1st ed.
        p.   cm.
    ISBN 0-9603924-9-1
        1. United States—Social life and customs—-1971-
2. Philadelphia Region (Pa.)—Social life and customs.
[1. United States—Social life and customs—1971-]
I. Weidner, Bea, ill. II. Title.
E169.04.S62 1995
973.92—dc20

Printed in the United States of America on acid free paper
    95   96   97   98   0 9 8 7 6 5 4 3 2
First edition

For Mother,
who bragged about me.

Contents

Foreword

J im Smart is a newspaper columnist, something I have wanted to be ever since I started reading *Evening Bulletin* columnists with names like Art Buchwald, Sandy Grady, James Reston, Claude Lewis, Drew Pearson and James Smart.

Of course, this was back in the days when Jim still had hair, which is exactly the kind of thing a newspaper columnist might say if he wanted to describe some vague near-distant past, while enjoying a joke at the expense of his subject, even if the joke has very little to do with the "reality" of the subject's follicular endowment, or in Jim's case, the lack thereof.

I bring up Jim's hair because it is perhaps the only insight I can offer into why he chose to name this book of his columns *"Soggy Shrub Rides again and other improbabilities."*

Long-time students of columns by Jim Smart —the so-called Smart Alex, whose namesake was Jim's first fan in the Italian Market, an employee at Claudio's House of Cheese nicknamed Alexander the Grate – will recognize the Smart eye at work in this book, the observed details that beg the cosmic questions few other writers have the courage (or gall) to ask.

Is the Grand Canyon a fake? Did Old Faithful ever cheat on Mrs. Faithful? Is Ingawa the Swahili word for Kemo Sabe? Were the Apostles the first to popularize mid-life career changes?

Let's face it, if it weren't for the Jim Smarts of this world, we wouldn't even know enough to question the obvious, let alone the obscure. Or as Jim might put it (and he did): "If a writer can't write about writing, what can he write about, right?"

He has also observed, "Just about everyone who ever lived is dead. Present company excepted." And "I haven't noticed myself getting grouchy as I get older. What I have noticed is that there's a lot more to complain about these days than there used to be."

What makes Jim Smart grouchy are the things that make him interesting. Why, he wonders, are Halloween decorations allowed in public schools and Christmas decorations aren't? Both are pagan festivals modified into Christian holidays.

Elsewhere Jim asks why every comment on TV news has to be a sound bite. "Columnists aren't limited to bites," he writes. "I can write a whole snack."

What you've got here is a smorgasbord of Smart snacks; some are salty, some are tart, and some are cuckoo as Cocoa Puffs. But each snack includes the minimum daily requirement of STTA (Something to Think About) or IDKT (I Didn't Know That!)

So start munching. Betcha can't eat just one.

Clark DeLeon
Long-time columnist and feature writer,
Philadelphia Inquirer

Introduction

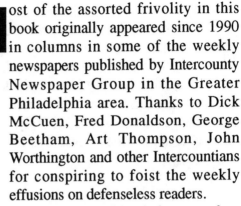

Most of the assorted frivolity in this book originally appeared since 1990 in columns in some of the weekly newspapers published by Intercounty Newspaper Group in the Greater Philadelphia area. Thanks to Dick McCuen, Fred Donaldson, George Beetham, Art Thompson, John Worthington and other Intercountians for conspiring to foist the weekly effusions on defenseless readers.

In rendering the former columns into book form, profuse thanks need to be heaped all over the likes of Joanne Dhody, Joe Nettis, Laurence Salzman, Bea Weidner , Clark DeLeon, and also the Unknown Thankee , the helpful person I forgot and whose feelings will thus be bruised.

Most thanks of all are directed at Barbara Torode, who has designed books for doctors, photographers, educators and other word-abusers, but this time braved the trauma of being married to the author.

The columns reprinted here often commented on suitably earth-shaking matters that, like most vital news more than a month old, are now quaint and dim memories. Timely topics decompose fast. To help current readers understand any passe references, a few slight changes have been made from some of the original versions, and some explanatory material has been wedged in here and there. In several instances, the original texts have been amended not for clarity, but for reasons more whimsical.

Loyal readers of the column (you know who you are) should also not be confused by the fact that one or two pieces in the book have not been in print before.

These essays occasionally include concepts specific to the

Philadelphia area. Readers in benighted regions beyond the rim of the Delaware Valley are requested to be tolerant when they come upon such obscurities.

All of these columns were constructed with tongue at half cheek. Readers with serious minds and tender sensibilities are asked to refrain from sending the author complaints that their favorite opinion has been disrepected, or that some jocularly distorted fact is not correct. This will save the author the cost of a postage stamp to send his reply, which would most likely be a polite suggestion to lighten up.

Discovering Ancient Information

Discovering is what scientists do for a living, so you can't blame them for keeping at it. But it might be nice if they laid off for a while, to give ordinary folks time to get used to the last things they discovered before they discover any new discoveries.

Latest News of 36,000 B.C.

Scientists recently announced some discoveries about stuff that was going on 38,000 years ago, give or take a couple of weeks.

One bunch of scientists discovered that Neanderthal persons were the ancestors of most white Europeans and Americans. Some others discovered that human beings were living in North America 38,000 years ago.

Until about 10 years ago, experts thought for years that Neanderthal folks were the ancestors of Europeans. Then some molecular biologists studied Neanderthal genes, and proclaimed that the Neanderthalers weren't anybody's ancestors, but had just sort of faded away, descendantless.

Now, the original discovery has been rediscovered, and there is going to be a big argument between the They're-Our-Ancestors scientists and the They-Are-Not-Either scientists.

This problem dates to 1856, when archaeologists poking around in a cave in the Neander Valley in Germany found the top of a skull belonging to a citizen who had just passed his 35,000th birthday. They decided that he was a different kind of person than they were used to, and everybody got excited.

Further digging turned up a lot of tools and things, and the archaeologists began figuring out how Neanderthal people lived.

Only about 30 Neanderthal skeletons were ever dug up. From this, the archaeologists were convinced that there was a big Neanderthal population. I'm not so sure about that reasoning. If they found $30 in my pocket, would that mean I have a whole lot of other money?

But I'm not an archaeologist, and never wanted to be one (it's hard, messy work, with all that digging) so what do I know?

Archaeologists also decided that Neanderthals were sophisticated enough to practice religion, citing the fact that they buried their dead. Is that really an indication of religion? I'll bet if a dead Neanderthal were lying around for a few days, even an atheist would want to bury him.

The new theory that Neanderthals are related to modern Europeans is backed up by an anthropologist at the University of Pennsylvania who compared teeth of the two groups. Teeth are said to play an important role in anthropology because they last longer than bones. Presumably this means that long after a Neanderthal gentleman's bones have disintegrated, scientists can still dig up his great big smile.

Meanwhile, in New Mexico, other archaeologists recently unearthed remains of stone hearths in a cave littered with bones of extinct tapirs and giant bisons. Radioactivity tests showed that the trash was 38,000 years old, indicating that humans were cooking dinner in North America about the same time the Neanderthals were going out of the ancestor business in Europe.

Until this discovery, the official date for the first

Americans to wander in from Asia was about 11,500 years ago.

The archaeologists said that, in the stone hearths, they found charred logs eight inches in diameter, bigger than could have been brought in by an animal.

That log-dragging proof doesn't impress me as much as the fireplace. A giant bison could drag an eight-inch log into a cave if it really wanted to. But if it then lit up a fire to char-broil some tapirburgers, the scientists really have a discovery.

Thanks for Nothing, Maya

A sales pitch came in the mail for a series of books about Lost Civilizations. The circular has color photographs of pyramids and mummies and other pieces of lost civilizations that nobody has lost yet, or else are sitting around in modern science's lost-and-found department.

There are lots of blurbs of information in the circular. I learned a lot from it. One thing I learned was that I can't afford the books.

A more interesting piece of knowledge was a mention that, beside carving fancy pictures on big stone stela and cutting the heart out of a human sacrifice now and then, the ancient Maya invented zero.

It seems unlikely that all of the Maya got together down at the pyramid one day and thought up zero. It's probable that one Maya mathematician, after experimenting with a whole bunch of other numbers that were discarded and remain unknown to this day, suddenly hit on zero, yelled the Pre-Columbian Guatemalan equivalent of "Eureka!" and ran out to impress all the other Maya math whizzes.

You would think that the fellow who invented zero would be world famous, like Newton, who discovered falling, or Einstein, who discovered relatives.

Maybe the reason we never heard of him was that he was extremely modest. Maybe when another Maya came up with chisel in hand and asked the mathematician to autograph his stela, and said, "I think it's really neat that you invented zero", the mathematician said, "Oh, it's nothing."

Did the ancient Maya have a patent office? Did the guy who invented zero try to register the idea? It must have been an interesting interview.

"What is this you've invented, sir?"

"It's a zero."

"What does it do?"

"Well, suppose you have a one. You put one of my zeros after it. Now it's a 10."

"Why?"

"What do you mean, why? It just is."

"Okay, suppose I take the one away from your, whatyacallit? Zero? Then what have I got?"

"You've got nothing."

"So you invented nothing."

"That's right."

"Is this a joke? Did Louie send you up here?"

The Maya disappeared, and there are zero of them left, but fortunately a few other geniuses also invented zero. And once people got used to zeros, they couldn't do without them. If there were no zeros, it would say $1 on a one dollar bill, $1 on a ten dollar bill and $1 on a hundred dollar bill. Working in a bank would become hell.

If there were no zeros, a football player who weighed 300 pounds would only weigh 3 pounds. If he gained a pound, he would weigh 31 pounds. If he gained ten pounds, he would still weigh 31 pounds.

If there were no zeros, the sun would be 92 miles away instead of 92,000,000 and we'd all get a heck of a sunburn. And 1992 would be only the 5th anniversary of Columbus coming to America.

When Columbus came, he brought zeros with him. I'll bet he was surprised to find that the Indians already had some.

Dead Leaders on Display

The Egyptian Museum in Cairo is planning to put the mummies of 11 pharaohs and pharaoh's wives on display for the first time in 14 years. Seti I and Ramses II are among the more popular pharaohs who will soon be lolling about for your inspection.

This is expected to make tourists very happy. There is nothing some folks like better than looking at Egyptians who have been dead for three or four thousand years.

The length of time they have been dead is important. Nobody but a few close friends and relatives want to look at your typical Egyptian who died last Monday. After an Egyptian has been dead long enough, he or she can become a museum exhibit.

Being a former pharaoh also helps make an Egyptian stiff an attraction. That goes also for pharaoh's wives, referred to here as pharaoh's wives because I don't know whether they were called pharaohess or pharaohette or Mrs. Pharaoh or what.

It probably doesn't matter, since we are communicating in English here and those ancient Egyptians all spoke hiero-glyphic.

The Egyptian Museum had a bunch of well-bandaged royal remains sitting around the premises years ago. Then Egypt's late President Anwar el-Sadat strolled through the museum one day in a thoughtful mood, and decided that it was posthumously undignified behavior for pharaohs to hang out there.

So the mummies were unexhibited in 1980.

But they will soon be dusted off and brought out again so that tourists will be willing to risk getting bombed on a bus by a Muslim fundamentalist in order to gawk at what little is left of Ramses II.

You'll notice that Mr. Sadat is not one of the former Egyptian leaders who will be put on display.

That points up how odd it is that tourists from Vermillion, South Dakota, or Cheektowaga, New York, travel to Cairo to see the dead bodies of ancient Egyptian leaders displayed in the Egyptian Museum.

Nobody would think of looking for the corpses of dead English kings in the British Museum. If anyone proposed removing George Washington or Thomas Jefferson or Rutherford B. Hayes from their resting places and propping them up on display at the Smithsonian, there would be much wailing and denouncing. Visiting famous but dead people in their burial place is accepted, but not in a museum. Except mummies.

Nor do horror movie producers make films about dead presidents rising from their graves and stalking around, strangling people and carrying pretty women in nightgowns off into the swamp.

You can make a movie about a mummy behaving that way, and nobody complains. Unless the Egyptians have complained but their statements were never properly translated from the hieroglyphic.

Another reason modern folks have grown so fond of ancient pharaohs is that they were rich. Their tombs tend to be gold plated and have all sorts of jewelry and expensive trinkets lying around. There's nothing like conspicuous wealth to make somebody a celebrity.

Maybe the American mummies that would attract tourists to museums would be Rockefellers and Vanderbilts and Astors. Or in the future, rock stars and running backs and relief pitchers. Or Perot I or Trump II.

Art Department

One thing artists and writers have in common. Sooner or later or frequently, they will tell some stranger at a social gathering that they paint or write, and the stranger will respond, "Oh. But what do you do for a living?"

Artists One-Up Writers Again

An advertisement in an architect's magazine offers "masterpiece re-creations" for sale by an art gallery in Florida.

"The masters of today re-creating the masterpieces of yesterday for the collection of tomorrow," the advertisement blurbs enthusiastically.

It promises "hand-painted museum quality re-creations", and is illustrated by a reproduction of one of Claude Monet's incessant paintings of water lilies.

As usual, we find here that artists can get away with activities that would get writers laughed at, if not sued or arrested.

If a writer advertised that he was re-creating masterpieces by Hemingway, Hawthorne, Shakespeare or Fanny Hurst, turning out handwritten copies of their actual manuscripts, and was selling them to collectors, the best reaction he would get would be ridicule.

Those of us who write for a living have long been aware that painters of pictures enjoy the upper end of a double standard. They get away with a lot.

If an artist wants to paint a picture of a landscape, he is allowed by custom to set up shop on a hillside overlooking the view he wants to put on canvas. He sits there with his easel and brushes and beret, and paints what he sees, and passersby think he is picturesque and oozing with aesthetics.

If a writer set up his typewriter or computer terminal on the hillside and started to describe the landscape in words, passersby would think he was a few participles short of a compound verb form.

A writer is expected to sit in his dismal garret and describe the landscape from memory.

Another inequity: Suppose an artist decides to produce a painting of a naked woman. (It seems to be a frequent decision among artists.)

The artist can call his neighborhood model rental agency, or Nudes R' Us, or wherever artists get those models, and tell the shipping department to send around a young woman who will disrobe and pose. It's totally socially acceptable.

But what if a writer wants to write a description of an unclad woman?

If a writer called a model agency, and the young woman arrived and saw him sitting at his typewriter, and he asked her to take off her clothes and pose while he wrote about her, she would probably sock him, intimate loudly that he was a pervert, and call the cops.

Again, the poor writer has to work from memory.

Why is it that artists are allowed to do things writers aren't?

Why is it that they can unabashedly advertise that they are making copies of masterpieces, and instead of being criticized for lack of originality and of semi-fraud, their efforts are advertised to architects and decorators so those professionals can provide clients with the best quality fake Monet renderings of water lily ponds?

Anybody want to buy a neatly typed manuscript of "Martin Chuzzlewit" in Dickens's own words? I can supply one cheap. And with even lower rates for Xerox copies.

Who Slugged Mona Lisa?

A fellow in Maryland claims to have evidence that Mona Lisa was a battered wife.

Mona Lisa was the missus of an Italian merchant named Giocondo, and Leonardo Da Vinci painted her portrait in about the year 1500. Leonardo stuck a wimpy little smile on her face, which for some reason has intrigued various portrait-watchers from the Renaissance until last week.

People wonder what caused that mysterious expression around Mona's mouth.

Now we have a new theory. Mona Lisa's famous smile may have resulted because Signor Giocondo busted her in the chops.

This smile analysis was advanced by one Joseph Borkowski, described in reports of his discovery as a "Maryland art expert and dentist."

"She isn't smiling," he was quoted as saying. "Her expression is typical of people who have lost their front teeth."

His study of Mrs. Giocondo's kisser also revealed signs of scar tissue around her mouth, the art expert and dentist announced.

His conclusion is that Mona Lisa's old man, on at least one occasion, let her have it right in the bocca.

There is no reason to doubt the powers of observation and reasoning of Dr. Borkowski. Art expert and dentist does not sound like an everyday combination of aptitudes. But then, Leonardo himself was an art expert, painter, sculptor, inventor, architect, musician, engineer, botanist, anatomist, astronomer, geologist, and just about everything but a dentist.

So art expert and dentist is a reasonable blend, even in Maryland where we might more likely expect to find a crab expert and dentist or a lacrosse player and dentist.

Nor can we suspect that Leonardo didn't give us a precise depiction of the condition of Mrs. Giocondo's labial region.

Not only was he one heck of a painter, but he had studied human anatomy up, down and sideways, dissecting every deceased Italian he could get his hands on. If anybody could do an accurate rendering of what was what in and around Mona's mouth, it was Leonardo.

So Dr. Borkowski may be right. If Leonardo had allowed Mona to give a nice big ear-to-ear, visitors to the Louvre might be staring into a toothless blank space under the poor girl's nose.

But hold on. Let's be fair. Just because Mona had her teeth knocked out doesn't mean that it was the late Signor Giocondo who was responsible.

Dr. Borkowski, and all other art experts and/or dentists, should give the poor guy the benefit of the doubt.

Mona could have been in a carriage accident and walloped her face on the dashboard. Even Leonardo hadn't thought to invent the air bag.

Or maybe she slipped on a spot of carelessly-spilled tomato sauce on the kitchen floor while carrying a platter of pasta she had lovingly prepared for her kind and gentle husband, and pitched forward and clobbered her chin on the pump handle.

Or could it have been Leonardo who socked her, because she wouldn't sit still while posing?

After nearly 500 years, it will take investigation by more than an art expert and dentist to find out who slugged Mona Lisa.

Political Correctness

There is a trend among intellectuals to discredit the ideas of anyone the intellectual in question disagrees with, particularly anyone who is too deceased to defend himself. This trend is called political correctness, probably because it would be politically incorrect to call it intolerence or stupidity.

The Posthumous Cold Shoulder

News reports from New Orleans say that the city is considering a policy to change the names of any schools named after "former slave owners or others who did not respect equal opportunity for all persons."

At the top of the hit list is a former slave owner named George Washington.

This is all part of the idea of "political correctness" that is being espoused by assorted policians, college professors, ethnic leaders and other self-anointed experts who devote their lives to telling the rest of us what it's all right to think.

One of their basic premises seems to be that people in the past should be vilified and given a posthumous cold shoulder because they didn't behave then the way we have decided we should behave now.

The seekers of political correctitude say that our diverse American society should question the cultural values of white Anglo-Saxon Protestants, whenever they can still find a few.

It will be useful if some of the currently uncorrect citizens among us can have their consciousnesses elevated a tad or two on the subject of racial, ethnic and other minority issues. But why pick on dead people?

Slavery existed since the first glimmerings of nastiness in the human race. That's no endorsement, but it should give the political correctors a clue that George Washington was just a human being stuck in the cultural values of his time, and of eons of time before that.

The correcticators want to lop poor General Washington's name off schools and institutions, because he didn't conform to human rights standards that were just beginning to seep into American consciousness about the time he went off to that big diverse culture in the sky.

While they're at it, they should demand that his name be erased from that double-decker highway bridge in New York, on the grounds that the General never drove an automobile. Obviously, he was anti-auto.

And they should take his name off the medical school at Washington University, because the general died of a strep throat and never once asked his doctor to give him antibiotics. Okay, so they didn't have that kind of medicine in 1799. They didn't have freedom for slaves, either, but we're talking correctness here.

It has been suggested that the Benjamin Franklin High School in Philadelphia and the one in New York should change their names because Ben once owned a slave.

Sure, sure, Ben Franklin decided that slavery was wrong, and became the first president of the Abolition Society. Sure, his last public act, while he was terminally ill at age 84, was to write a tract denouncing slavery.

But it isn't politically correct to reform. A person has to be born agreeing with the politicians, professors and purifiers, or his name should be stricken from the history books. Furthermore, he has to conform to all future opinions of how he should have behaved.

How strange that preachers of ethnic tolerance promote intolerance of dead WASPs. And how strange that their deceased but incorrect targets, slave owners and all, originated the very political system that allows them the unique freedom to denounce anybody they decide is unworthy. Which is likely to be anybody but the denouncers themselves — dead or alive.

Watch Those Long Sentences

Naomi Wolf, feminist author of "The Beauty Myth," visited a college campus and got accosted by some feminist students whose political correctness has been stretched well beyond femininitude.

One young woman accused Ms. Wolf of being elitist because she used a lot of compound sentences in her books.

Another female student asked Ms. Wolf if the act of writing a book isn't in itself exclusionary to women who can't read.

I am unable to guess how Ms. Wolf feels about this encounter, since I am a man and therefore modern culture no longer allows me to operate my brain in any manner that might approximate that of members of another sex, not to mention any brains belonging to persons who differ from me in ethnic, racial, religious, age, education level, hair style, hobby, dietary preference, zip code, or other important distinction.

(Although I also write long compound sentences.)

But Ms. Wolf is a graduate of Yale University, which has been turning out creators of elaborate compound sentences since 1701, so a male mind might dare to assume that she was a bit shocked to hear that using a subordinate clause or two here and there makes her unacceptable to the new breed of campus intellectual.

This kind of thinking (academia claims to believe that it's thinking) is something new in collegiate circles.

Before the political correctors slithered onto the scene, I often found myself, in various jobs through the years, working with persons who hold assorted graduate degrees from esteemed and ivy-infested halls of learning but are able to produce clear declarative sentences only by lucky accident.

Nevertheless, many business executives afflicted with large doses of higher education believe that the more complicated and circumlocutious a sentence, the more elegant and important it sounds. They like their sentences like their automobiles, long, dark and unnecessarily powerful.

Not the current campus dwellers. They like sentences short. Or so Ms. Wolf's experience would indicate. It's astonishing.

So is the second complaint. The logic is so pure. The truth is so unarguable. Writing books insults the illiterate.

The next logical step as our universities slide cheerily into the nirvana of political correctness is to ban reading from the classroom. This will place everyone on a level academic playing field, and allow even the Beavises and Buttheads of this great nation the God-given privilege of attending a hallowed institution like Yale, Hocking Tech, McNeese State or the Palmer College of Chiropractic.

Reading, after all, was the invention of long-deceased white European males.

They invented compound sentences, too.

And have those socially-aware students noticed that Ms. Wolf's latest book, "Fire With Fire," costs $21? In addition to excluding the non-readers among us, she and her publishers (each and every one probably a man) have callously excluded poor women.

It's all part of the ongoing male plot to keep women subjugated. You don't see those nasty compound sentences in cook books.

Westward Ho (Ho Ho)

Americans who live in the East are fascinated by books and movies about Western folks like cowboys and gunfighters, but folks who live in the West have shown little interest in books and movies about Eastern folks like plumbers and stock brokers.

How the West was Fabricated

 It was reported that the U. S. Geological Survey spent $6,000 to buy some fake rocks to put in the Grand Canyon.

The two five-foot boulders they bought are made of polyester resins and fiberglass.

This government purchase would seem as unnecessary as the House of Representatives buying a couple of plastic Congressmen to prop up at desks in the Capitol. It would seem that there are more than enough real rocks and real Congressmen already taking up space in the Grand Canyon and Washington, respectively.

The fake boulders were made to fit over the equipment of a water sampling station on Havasu Creek, which flows into the Colorado River in the Grand Canyon. The Geological Surveyors felt that the sight of water-sampling paraphernalia would take something away from the scenery, and decided to disguise the whole works.

Or so they claim. This raises some immediate suspicions.

We caught them moving two fake boulders into the area. For all we know, all of the rocks out there are fakes.

The whole National Park might be a fake. Maybe the Grand Canyon was dug out in a secret government project.

Maybe they excavated that big hole because they wanted to send a zillion tons of dirt to Iran in exchange for hostages or something. Iran could use some good topsoil.

Any cash Iran put up to buy all that dirt probably was used by the CIA to build polyester and fiberglass boulders to be dropped on some army we didn't like in Central America.

Most of that stuff out West doesn't look real. Fess up, now; does the idea of Old Faithful ring true to you? Do you really believe that natural water squirts out of the ground every so often right on schedule so tourists can take pictures of it?

Let's face it. If it weren't for those fancy tourist attractions, no rational Eastern person would ever bother to travel hundreds of miles to visit those flat, dried up, hot, dusty Western states. The government may have had to rig up all of that improbable scenery to lure the sightseers.

The government probably painted the Painted Desert, petrified the Petrified Forest, salted the Salt Lake and imported those dumb bears to Yellowstone. For all we know, the whole darn Rocky Mountains are made of polyester resins and fiberglass.

Most likely, the entire development of the travel industry out West was handled on a secret federal contract by the Walt Disney people. Those giant faces on Mount Rushmore sure smack of Disney, don't they? They're probably made of fiberglass. I guess we're lucky that they don't keep singing "It's a large world, after all" over and over.

Next time I happen to be passing the Grand Canyon on my way over to the 7-Eleven for milk, I'm going to get out and kick a few boulders and see if they give out a hollow thump.

If I accidentally pick one of the few real rocks, the yell I let out on the subject of my injured toe will create a nice rich echo up and down that big phony ditch they try to persuade everybody is a canyon.

Look Out for That Canyon

A disturbing issue I tracked throughout 1993 was that six tourists were killed by falling into the Grand Canyon.

I don't mean to make light of a serious situation. (That is what you're obliged to say before making light of a serious situation.)

But it seems to me that the Grand Canyon, in its worst moments, is large enough that anyone strolling along should notice it. Tourists, who travel to the area specifically expecting to see a rather deep canyon around someplace, should have foreseen the possibility of coming upon it.

We can exempt from this criticism the guy who fell in while having his photograph taken. Any amateur photographer who has ever said "Step back a little, Aunt Maude, so I can get all of you in the picture," knows how it could happen.

Someone has suggested that the mules who frequent the Grand Canyon vicinity in large numbers, providing uncomfortable transportation and obnoxious outcries, tend to leave behind quantities of slippery material that might be responsible for some of the unexpected descents into the canyon.

In Hong Kong in 1993, the city opened a half-mile-long escalator designed to carry 26,000 commuters per day up and down a 450 foot slope. Would something like that help eliminate both the falling and the mules at the Grand Canyon?

Soggy Shrub Rides Again

A new book reveals the answers to more than 1,000 questions frequently asked by patrons of the New York Public Library.

An advertisement for the book claims that one of those questions is, "What does kemo sabe mean?"

Kemo sabe, as every literate person knows, is what the Lone Ranger was called by his Faithful Indian Companion, Tonto.

And according to the New York Public Library, in the Navajo language kemo sabe means "soggy shrub".

This is a shocking revelation.

Now, I have never been a Daring and Resourceful Masked Rider of the Plains, and have no immediate plans to become one, since there is very little demand for that kind of work

these days. But if I were in the Masked Rider business and caught my most trusted employee constantly referring to me as Soggy Shrub, he would find himself on the unemployment line back at the reservation quicker than you could say "Hi Yo, Silver."

This is the second time in my life that a foreign phrase uttered by a boyhood hero has been exposed as totally disappointing when translated.

In the old Tarzan movies, Johnny Weissmuller used to yell ingawa a lot. He'd holler ingawa at an elephant while he was riding on the poor critter's head and kneeing it viciously behind the ears because he was in a hurry to rescue Jane from some evil ivory hunters with pith helmets and slick mustaches.

Ingawa sounded like a command of heroic urgency.

Then one day I met a man from Kenya who taught a

course in Swahili in the Philadelphia public schools. I asked him what ingawa means.

"It means 'even though'," he said with a grin.

Ingawa, it seems, is a connective that pops up in everyday Swahili conversation so frequently that a foreigner listening to a couple of East Africans on the street corner might think it is a very important word. In the same way, somebody who doesn't speak English might pick out a phrase like "you know" or "I mean" being repeated by somebody overheard talking around, I mean, like, you know, here.

So Tarzan would drop from a tree onto an elephant's head, while the background music swelled dramatically in preparation for a pachydermous gallop through the under-brush (and probably some overbrush, too) and the Lord of the Apes would shout to the great, lumbering beast: "Even though!"

Nah. It just doesn't work.

There might be some rationale to Tonto slyly referring to the Lone Ranger as Soggy Shrub. All observers of the Ranger's methods of operation were aware that whenever there was something peculiar happening in town, the Masked Man always sent poor Tonto in to do the dangerous espionage work.

If the bad guys got wise that they were under surveillance and decided to use Tonto for six-shooter practice, old Soggy Shrub would be safe back at the campfire, heating up some buffalo stew.

Being used as the advance man for a gun battle could have evoked some disrespectful feelings in Tonto when addressing the boss. And he could have called him something worse, I suppose. Even though (or ingawa) it's possible, cultural differences being unpredictable, that the worst thing a Navajo can call a Masked Rider of the Plains is Soggy Shrub.

Any Old Time Religion

This section is courageously included in the book, risking its banishment from public schools, public libraries, public rest rooms and any other facilities that are protected by the Constitution from anything religious occurring there.

Shall We Gather at the Car Lot?

City officials in Burlington, N.J., were very upset when a newly-formed church congregation, not yet able to afford its own building, began holding Sunday services and Sunday School inthe showroom of an automobile dealer who is a church member.

The government leaders declared worshipping in a car dealership illegal, saying they didn't want to set a precedent of permitting businesses to allow religious and social activities on their properties.

The zoning board chairman was quoted as fretting that "even a bar could open a building for church services on a Sunday."

You can see the dangers in this.

Just let a bunch of saloons start holding Sunday School classes on Sunday, instead of respectably peddling booze as they do the other six days of the week, and who knows where it would lead.

Next thing you know, drug dealers would be preaching and testifying on their usual corners on Sundays. Burglars would be breaking into houses on Sundays and leaving religious tracts. Armed hold-up men would be barging into 7-Elevens on Sundays and forcing the clerks to memorize scripture verses.

You can't have people indiscriminately acting religious all over the place on Sunday. They should be forced to be religious inside churches where they don't bother anybody.

The reason that the auto showroom is available for such anti-social activity as Sunday School is that for nearly 40 years it has been illegal in New Jersey to sell automobiles on Sunday. Clearly, that law can't have anything to do with religion, or it would also forbid Jews, Muslims and Seventh Day Adventists to sell cars on Saturday.

Or is it possible that the law against Sunday sales of cars traces back to the Ten Commandments, which order us to keep the Sabbath Day holy? If so, it might be sensible to make it compulsory to hold religious services in automobile showrooms on Sunday, rather than forbid it.

What is allowable on the Sabbath is not a new question. Some local officials in the Holy Land tried to blow the whistle on Jesus and his disciples when they were seen picking some grain in a field they were walking through and nibbling it on the Sabbath. That may not be relevant, because those were the days when everybody agreed that Saturday was the day you were supposed to keep holy. And there have been very few complaints about Sunday grain-nibbling in Burlington lately.

The grain-picking incident was described by St. Matthew, one of the alleged culprits, and he was a public official himself. He was never head of the zoning board, that I know of, but he started out as a tax collector. Becoming an apostle was one of those mid-life career changes.

I doubt that St. Matthew could conceive of a city official

claiming that having religious services in a commercial property was a violation of the law requiring business to close on Sunday.

It seems to me that having religious services in a tax-paying commercial property should please municipal officials more than having them in the typical non-taxpaying church.

At this writing, the congregation has an appeal of the zoning decision before a county court. Meanwhile, maybe there are some catacombs under Burlington, N.J., where these Christians can hide out on Sundays if necessary.

Time to Honor the Bad Guys

On November 1, All Saints Day is observed. The evening before that day is Halloween, which tradition dedicates to ghosts and witches and all the evil, sinful things that are the opposite of saints.

Because of All Saints Day, people naturally decorate their houses at this time of year with pictures of saints and religious symbols signifying goodness, and children get dressed up as saints and holy figures and go about giving gifts and doing good.

What's that you say? It doesn't work that way? All the decorations and costuming and behavior are in honor of the horrible and evil things that infest the world the night before All Saints Day? Well, that's hard to believe.

Yet it seems to be true. Halloween is the holiday when we honor the bad guys.

This business about Halloween can mostly be blamed on the Druids. They were ancient pagan priests who hung around on both sides of the English Channel, long long ago, before there was an All Saints Day, before there was printing, before there was gunpowder, before there was peanut butter, before there was golf, almost even before George Burns.

The Druids understood many mysteries. They had an autumn festival called Samhain. They pronounced it "SAH-win." One of the mysteries Druids understood was how to pronounce things funny.

All respectable Druids believed that on or about that night in autumn, all the ghosts, witches and demons came out from wherever they are the rest of the time, and messed around a lot. The Druids also believed that cats are former bad human beings who have been changed into their current form as a punishment for their sins. The behavior of your average cat would substantiate this theory.

Some year in the eighth century, the Pope named Nov. 1 as All Saints Day. And the night of Oct. 31 the next year, a bunch of kids showed up at the door of St. Peter's yelling "Trick or treat!" in Latin.

And so the pagan customs of the season were transferred to All Saints Day, in the same way pagan concepts like eggs and bunnies were hooked up with Easter and pagan concepts like evergreen trees and mistletoe and Toys R Us with Christmas.

One of the nice things about Halloween decorations is that they are Constitutional. There are schools and courthouses and city halls and jails and other public buildings all over the U. S. of A. that don't hang up religious symbols around Christmas or Easter, because the Constitution says that we are all free to practice our religions in our own way as long as nobody notices.

But the people who are afraid that somebody might let something religious slip out (which happens often, God knows) have not yet caught on that Halloween is a contraction of All Hallows Evening, hallows being another way to say saints if you feel like it. They don't know that Halloween has anything to do with religion.

So it is still all right to hang up pictures of witches in public school rooms. But no saints, please.

Witches Have an Image Problem

An organization of people who say they are witches demanded recently that a school district in California remove the fairy tale "Hansel and Gretel" from its schools. The witches complained that the story gives children the impression that witches are socially unacceptable and that a proper way to deal with them is to shove them into ovens and render them into gingerbread.

Special interest groups often assail schools for allowing on the premises books they feel disparage their racial, ethnic, religious, occupational or other claim to uniqueness.

And fairy tales have been criticized in the past for possibly stimulating violence. Who knows how many school children, after reading "Little Red Riding Hood" or "The Three Little Pigs," have been incited to launch vicious and unprovoked assaults on innocent wolves?

But this may have been the first time that a pressure group like witches has expressed outrage.

The witches have a sound point. Fairy tales can generate negative images.

Giants, for instance, are always shown in a bad light. In real life, few of them ever say, "Fee, fie, fo, fum" and the most antisocial activity they engage in is forming basketball teams.

Stepmothers and stepsisters also get a bad rap. Their titles are almost always preceded by the adjective "wicked."

And while racial protests have rightly eradicated "Little Black Sambo" from the classroom, nobody has noticed that in the same book, it was tigers who were the villains. Where are the animal rights advocates to complain that the tigers were portrayed as cold-blooded killers, an image they've been trying to live down for years?

Some fairy tales have a few socially redeeming qualities. Perhaps an organization of prince charmings (or is the plural princes charming?) will come forward to speak on behalf of the tales of Snow White and Cinderella.

In those two stories, we have instructive examples of faithfulness, nice girls finishing first, tolerance for short people and the benefits of being a great kisser.

Shakespeare also wrote some things that give a bad impression of witches. Maybe those witches in California should try to ban his works, too. The three witches who messed with Macbeth's mind are particularly notorious. But Shakespeare portrayed Joan of Arc as a witch, and she has since been made a saint, which should please witches everywhere.

It's interesting that the worried witches felt they had to petition the school board to remove the offending books. Wouldn't you expect witches just to throw a few extra newt eyes in the cauldron, mutter some arcane phrases and make the books disappear from the shelves in a puff of sulphurous smoke?

That would take care of things for a spell.

There's another way for the California witches to handle the school book problem.

All they have to do is convince every American school board that witchcraft is a religion, a claim modern witches often make. If the public school leaders think the books have anything to do with religion, they will cite the First Amendment and toss the offending works out at once.

Take Me Out
to You-Know-Where

It's astonishing how many persons, particularly women, immigrants and holders of advanced Ivy League degrees, do not understand the overwhelming importance of baseball. Such confused persons may find the following helpful.

An Overview of Baseball

Professional baseball is a game played by groups of young millionaires. They are watched by crowds of people who yell a lot, whenever yelling does not interfere with drinking beer.

Baseball is committed by two teams of about 25 athletes, who each send nine of their number onto a field of green plastic stuff in a stadium. The enthusiastic onlookers then shout demands that they perform home runs, double plays, pick-offs at second, Texas leaguers and other mysterious rituals.

Players not actively engaged in these esoteric activities sit on a long bench in a depressed enclosure, discussing sex and/or their investments.

The sitting players are required by custom to chew. Some chew tobacco, others bubble gum and still others sunflower seeds.

The teams keep playing until one of them wins.

The above is all the average person needs to know about baseball.

History of the Game

Modern baseball was invented in 1835 by Abner Doubleday. Yelling and beer drinking had been invented previously by other people.

After he invented baseball, Doubleday enrolled at West Point. What else could he do for an encore after creating an entire National Pastime?

Doubleday was in command of the Third Division, First Corps of the United States Army at the Battle of Gettysburg. That means he was a Yankee general.

Today, most Americans would be more impressed if he had been a Yankee outfielder. They may have something there.

A Yankee outfielder named Babe Ruth was probably never anywhere near Gettysburg unless he stopped in at a saloon there once, yet most people know him better than they know Abner Doubleday.

Babe Ruth hit so many home runs that everybody thinks somebody named a candy bar after him, although the candy bar was really named for President Grover Cleveland's baby, Ruth. Her home run hitting abilities are not highly regarded.

Some experts say that Abner Doubleday devised and named the game of baseball in 1839, not 1835. Others say he didn't do it at all.

Some of the antiDoubledayites say Alexander J. Cartwright really invented baseball in 1845 (except for those who say Cartwright did it in 1846).

Somebody must have made up the rules sometime, because by 1869 people were taking the game so seriously that in Cincinnati, they decided to start paying their players.

They paid Harry Wright, a jeweler from Philadelphia, the astounding sum of $1,200 for the year to manage the club and play center field. The other players also received excessive remuneration.

The investment was worthwhile. The Cincinnati Red

Stockings racked up an 1869 season of 56 wins and one tie.

Aaron Champion announced at that time that he would rather be president of the Red Stockings than president of the United States. Since he was president of the Red Stockings, things worked out nicely. The opinion of President Ulysses S. Grant on the subject has not been recorded.

The first professional baseball league was organized in 1871, which gave the gatherings of spectators the opportunity to see the Philadelphia Athletics play renowned teams like the Fort Wayne Kekiongas or the Brooklyn Eckfords while yelling and drinking beer.

From those modest beginnings, we have reached the point in history where young men join teams whose names pay homage to favorite birds or the color of their socks, and are paid millions of dollars because they can understand the intricacies of such mysteries as the infield fly rule and balks. These technicalities become clear to the nonprofessional onlookers only after considerable effort is put into the yelling and the drinking of beer, particularly the latter.

Baseball Management Theory

Every baseball season, a few teams descend into an unpopular position that the baseball experts describe as "below .500", a condition often accompanied by being "in the cellar." This is accomplished by losing more games than they win.

Persons unfamiliar with sport might think that poor performance by a team would be blamed on the 25 alleged baseball players, or some of them.

It doesn't work that way. If the supposed athletes are throwing baseballs where comrades should be waiting to catch them, but aren't, or are hitting balls where opposing players are waiting to catch them, instead of elsewhere, it is not their fault.

It's the manager's fault. When athletes muddle up, the public often suggests in the rudest terms that the manager be fired.

Firing the manager is a time-honored practice. Take, for example, Charlie Stuart, better known to sports fans everywhere as King Charles I. He was managing the Royalists in the British League back in the 17th century.

The Royalists were up against some tough contenders for the pennant that season: the Roundheads, the Puritans, the Presbyterians, the Levelers, the Cavaliers and Parliament.

Well, the Royalists fell below .500, and Charlie got replaced by a manager named Ollie Cromwell. (Actually, they cut off Charlie's head, but that isn't often done these days. People are more cruel now; they force the former manager to coach third base•instead, or send him to manage a quadruple-A team in Mulespit, Missouri.)

Giant corporations operate the same way. The crack marketing team at General Scribbling Instruments Corp. spends $7.3 million on research and development of a double-barreled fountain pen for use by Siamese twins. The new product sells only 14 units, despite heavy advertising, and the losses cause the company's stock price per share to drop from $57 to the point where 10 shares can be traded for a Ferris Fain baseball card.

So do the directors fire the marketing team? No. They fire the Chief Executive Officer.

And remember when they brought in Jerry Ford to manage after Dick Nixon's team went under .500? That's how the system works.

Ready to Turn This Century?

We are in the waning years of the 20th century, which is nice for those interested in waning. As we creep closer to the year 2000, all sorts of arguments will start about the turn of the century. The following information will not settle them. Too bad.

How We Got Calendared

There will be much whooping and carrying on when December 31, 1999, comes along, because the next day will begin the year 2000, a radical change after all the years we've experienced that begin with a 19.

But that won't be the turn of the century.

There was no year zero. The first year, calendarily speaking, was Year Number One. The first century ended in 100.

So this century will end in 2000. The next century will begin in 2001. That seems obvious to anyone who's into arithmetic, but there are legions of calendar aficionados who disagree, and will argue violently on the subject.

The measuring of years and centuries and other artificial chunks of time has caused lots of confusion through the aforementioned years and centuries.

The Babylonians, Egyptians, Aztecs, and other ancient people who liked to pay attention, devised dandy ways to keep track of passing years, but they weren't sure what number year it really was. It's nice to live in an civilized era when we know positively that this is the number of year it is, and not some other number. We can just look on any calendar, and the year is printed right there.

We owe a lot of our calendarizing ideas to the old Romans. They counted years from what they said was the year Rome was founded. They started out enjoying years with 10 months, and only 304 days. They seemed to know there should be another 60 days tucked in there someplace, but they just ignored the subject and hoped nobody would notice.

As the years went by, the Roman government stuck a couple of extra months at the beginning of the year, because taxes were collected by the month, and more months brought in more taxes. Let's hope nobody in Washington stumbles onto that notion.

After a while, this tinkering had seasons arriving in different months than they used to, which sensitive Romans found bothersome.

In the Roman year 709, Julius Caesar got it into his head to whip up a better calendar. The year 709 in Rome was what we call 46 B. C. You would have had a hard time convincing Julius that it was 46 B. C., but it was.

He hired a Greek astronomer named Sosigenes to design a calendar. The two of them came up with a year that had 12 months of 31 and 30 days, except for February, which had 29.

To get the new calendar up and running, Julius ruled that 46 B. C. would have 445 days. The Romans called that "the year of confusion." They called it that in Latin, but that didn't make it any less confusing.

Two years later, Julius was assassinated while entering the capitol and died of 20 stab wounds in the rotunda. It isn't clear whether the guys who did it were still mad about the calendar change.

While Sosigenes was at it, he had figured out that it takes the earth 365 and a quarter days to go around the sun, and worked out the idea that every fourth year needs an extra day.

We still believe him on that one.

Then, 578 years later, a monk named Dionysius Exiguus started insisting that the year he was in was 532, dating from the year he computed that Christ was born, which he christened Year One, abbreviated A. D. in places monks hung out.

The Venerable Bede, also a monk by trade, complained in A. D. 730 that the Sosigenes year was 11 minutes and 14 seconds too long, adding up to an error of about a day every 28 years. Nobody bothered doing anything about that for more than 800 years. Would you have?

By 1582, the errors had accumulated so much they got on Pope Gregory XIII's nerves. He decreed that the day after Oct. 4 would be Oct. 15, getting rid of those pesky extra days. Some people got upset about that, but what fun is it being a pontiff if you can't abolish some days here and there every so often?

After that deft correction, we still would gain three days every 400 years. So one of every four years ending in 00 is now a leap year. The year 1600 was a leap year; 1700, 1800 and 1900 were not, but 2000 will be.

The British government in 1582 was inclined to ignore suggestions from Pope Gregory. Queen Elizabeth I was running things. Her daddy had disagreed nastily with three popes in a row, and she was not enthusiastic about papal thoughts on calendar revision.

It wasn't until 1752 that the British decided to adopt the calendar we now all know and love. King George II mandated that the day after Sept. 2 would be Sept. 14, which straightened things out neatly. He also moved New Years Day from March 25 to January 1. Both Julius Caesar and Pope Gregory XIII had already done that, but it's hard to get an Englishman to change his mind.

To work out the New Years Day shift, King George let 1752 start on March 25 as usual, and ended it on Dec. 31. This meant that there was no January, February or a large hunk of

March designated as belonging to 1752. A baby born in February, 1751 became one year old 12 months later, in February, 1753. British citizens got quite disconcerted when 11 September days and more than two winter months were cancelled. But kings used to do things like that.

All of this shows how complicated the calendar business always has been. So if arguments start about whether the century will end in 1999 or 2000, it's no wonder.

Looking Backward

Writing about history has advantages. George Washington has never called up and complained that he was misquoted. So far.

Pilgrims Get All the Publicity

Every October, William Penn's birthday passes by and very few people notice, even in Pennsylvania and New Jersey, although he was in charge of colonial New Jersey for a while and founded Pennsylvania, and residents of those states would most likely be living in a place named something else if it weren't for him.

Every November, everybody gets all excited about celebrating the anniversary of a bunch of folks in New England having a turkey dinner.

The Pilgrims must have had a good publicity agent. William Penn was nice to the Indians all the time, and hardly anybody thinks about him. The Pilgrims invited the Indians over for dinner once, and it became a national holiday.

William Penn founded Pennsylvania as a Quaker colony where all inhabitants were free to worship in their own way, and let them do it (although atheists weren't allowed to vote, but even Quakers had to draw the line someplace.)

The Pilgrims came to Massachusetts to be free to worship in their own way, and to make sure that everybody did worship in the Pilgrims' own way, they hanged an occasional Quaker who was passing through. God knows what they did to atheists.

The Pilgrims started out as Puritans, who were a group of people who wanted to purify the Church of England. The church was perfectly happy the way it was, and the authorities tried to explain that to the Puritans by throwing them in jail and seizing their property and otherwise trying to get their attention.

One group of Puritans lived in a village called Scrooby, and decided to leave. With a mailing address like Scrooby, who could blame them?

In 1608, they fled to Holland. But their kids started speaking Dutch, which was almost as disturbing as living in a place called Scrooby or getting locked up, so they bought a ship called the Mayflower and sailed to America.

And in November of 1620, they arrived in Massachusetts and saw a rock and decided to step on it and make it famous.

After that, they spent a good deal of time starving, and proved to be very good at it. But the local Indians, who were annoyed enough at having a mob of Europeans wandering around wearing funny hats and carrying Bibles and chopping down big chunks of forest, didn't want to have a few dozen starving Pilgrims on their hands.

So the Indians taught the Pilgrims how to plant corn and what to do with turkey leftovers and all sorts of woodland lore, and when the Pilgrims managed to unstarve themselves, they invited the Indians to drop by for Thanksgiving dinner.

The celebration lasted for three days. The Pilgrims were probably looking at their watches and yawning, but the Indians just kept sitting around and talking and asking somebody to pass the cranberries.

The Pilgrims called the place Plymouth, and there you go again. Nobody named an automobile after any of William Penn's places.

Does the Prince Eat His Veggies?

An advertisement for vitamins in a health magazine proclaimed that King Henry VIII died not of his vices and excesses as is commonly thought, but because he didn't eat his vegetables.

Portraits of Henry VIII show a big-bellied, no-neck guy who doesn't look like he lived on salads, so the no-vegetable theory is no surprise.

As for the excess and vice theory, Henry had six wives at one time or another, which probably qualifies as excess. And he beheaded two of them and divorced two, which adds up to vice at the very least.

History books don't say a lot about how many vegetables Henry consumed.

There is one 16th century mention that his third wife, Jane Seymour, died in childbirth "through the fault of them that were about her, who suffered her to take great cold and to eat things that her fantasy in sickness called for." If the servants were bringing poor dying Jane pizza and Haagen-Dazs and french fries and stuff when she called for them, instead of forcing down broccoli and carrots and alfalfa sprouts, it's quite likely they were letting the king ignore the basic food groups, too.

Leaping forward 445 years or so, I've seen no information about Queen Elizabeth II's consumption of vegetables, or lack thereof.

But lately, not eating his vegetables is one of the few things her son Charles hasn't been accused of.

All of the publications that pant over the doings of celebrities claim that Prince Charles ignores his wife and children, goes off hunting and playing polo while the Mrs. sits around the castle brooding, blatantly fools around with the wife of a courtier, and generally acts like... acts like...

Good golly! He's acting like a king of England.

All the way back to Ethelred the Unready, or even as far as Athelstan the Glorious, your average English king or prince kicked his wife and kids around a bit, ignored the queen while he sported, had a mistress or two or 27, and otherwise behaved the way Prince Charles does now.

The last king named Charles, who did his kinging a bit over 300 years ago, ignored his wife, too. He spent a lot of time fishing and at the races.

He also had a bunch of expensive mistresses, including two famous actresses and several court ladies. He had 13 illegitimate children.

The tabloids haven't caught our current Charles up to anything that elaborate yet. But his behavior is traditional.

His mother seems to have avoided scandal, as queens and princesses usually do. His grandpop, George VI, had a good reputation, but he started out in the navy, so he could have been up to something in several ports.

Charlie's Great-Uncle Edward VIII had a few love affairs as prince, including two with American divorcees, before he fell for twice-divorced Mrs. Simpson from Baltimore and went out of the king business to marry her.

Great-grandfather George V was a navy man, too, and there was a scandal about a girl friend on Malta. He also was prone to using salty language.

Great-great-grandfather Edward VII got caught with an actress in his tent while on military maneuvers when he was 19. He had six well-known mistresses (and one wife), was corespondent in a divorce, got in trouble for illegal gambling and ate five full-course meals a day (not all vegetables.)

So Prince Charles is just living up to established standards. The British press, People magazine and Princess Diana shouldn't be so surprised.

Cities by Any Other Name

Cities in the Soviet Union have gone into a frenzy of name-changing since the people over there decided to deMarx themselves and unLeninize.

St. Petersburg is calling itself St. Petersburg again. Czar Peter the Great named the town after his namesake saint back in 1703, but he was under the influence of German culture and called it a burg, German style.

That stuck until World War I, when Germans weren't admired any longer, so the Russians made the place a grad, which is Russian for burg, and it became Petrograd.

When the Bolsheviks took over, they wanted to keep the grad part but dump the saint part, and in 1924 they made it Leningrad. Now, Lenin's name is mudski, and the citizens voted to change it back to St. Petersburg.

About a dozen Soviet cities have readopted their old names. Gorky, renamed for a Marxist writer, has gone back to Nizhniy Novogorod. Andropov, renamed for the premier who ran things before Gorbachev, is Rybinsk again.

And Sverdlosk wants to return to being Ekaterinburg, which was named for Catherine the Great. Sverdlosk was said to be the executioner who shot the Czar and his family in that city in 1918, and his popularity seems to have worn off.

But renaming cities is nothing new.

For instance, the Dutch called it New Amsterdam when they started to put together a town on Manhattan Island in 1625. But a British fleet showed up in the harbor in 1664 and suggested that the place really should be renamed New York in honor of the Duke of York, King Charles II's brother. The British were such amiable people, and had such big cannons, that the Dutch cheerfully agreed.

Or there was the ancient city of Byzantium. Emperor Constantine I changed it to Constantinople in the A. D. 300s. In 1453, the Turks grabbed the city and called it Istanbul, although the name wasn't made official until 1930. A couple of years later, a songwriter named Jimmy Kennedy wrote a hit tune on the subject, concluding, "Why did Constantinople get the works? It's nobody's business but the Turks," which seems to settle that.

Or consider what happened to Stanleyville.

The Belgians took charge of the Congo in the middle of Africa for a long while, and named a city for Henry Morton Stanley, a reporter for the New York Herald who clumped through the jungle in 1869 trying to find Dr. David Livingstone, who didn't think he was lost.

(Stanley, himself, had changed his name from John Rowlands, but he wasn't a city, so let's leave him out of this.)

Well, that neighborhood of the Congo is called Zaire now, and in 1966 the name of Stanleyville was changed to Kisangani. It was probably the only city in the world named for a newspaper reporter, and I hated to see it go.

Why did Stanleyville disappear? It's nobody's business but Zaire.

Celebrating the Quincentennial

The year 1992 was a big deal as years go, because it was the 500th anniversary of Christopher Columbus wandering into the Western Hemisphere and discovering a whole bunch of real estate which a grateful world almost immediately named after Americo Vespucci instead of after Columbus.

There were all kinds of observations and celebrations and ceremonies and other disturbances all over the United States and in Spain, the Caribbean, South America and many other parts of the world, although there were a few people here and there who were not only indifferent, but in many cases loudly expressed the wish that Chris had hung a wrong left, wound up in the Antarctic by mistake and become an ice cube.

Many Native Americans, for instance, insist that they would be just as happy if Columbus had stayed home in Genoa where he was born, and followed his old man in the wool combing profession, and never got a notion to discover anything.

But when he was a small boy, Columbus got this peculiar idea that the world was round.

According to my third grade teacher, little Chris used to sit on the dock and watch the ships disappear over the horizon and think that when he grew up, he was going to be the captain of a ship that disappeared over the horizon, instead of wanting to be a fireman or a salami stuffer or whatever else more conservative Genoese kids wanted to be in those days.

Young Chris would say, "Some day I'm going to sail west to get to the east," and his mother would say, "Why don't you go out and play?"

Round worlds were not a popular item at that time. You had fellows like Lactantius Firmianus, an advisor to Emperor Constantine the Great, who once had raised the solid question, "Can there be a place on earth where things are upside down, where the trees grow downward, and the rain, hail and snow fall upward?"

People tended to pay attention to thinkers like Firmianus. But you'll notice that there is no Firmianus, Ohio, and no Firmianus Circle in Manhattan, so you can see where his arguments got him.

Meanwhile, Christopher Columbus grew up and went to Spain. I forget why. Most of us do the former, while the latter is optional.

He hung around on the doorstep of King Ferdinand and Queen Isabella, trying to pester them into paying for some ships so he could head west and see if he could bump into India or China or someplace.

The king and queen kept him waiting for seven years because they were busy persecuting the Muslims and the

Jews, and persecuting can take up all of your time.

Finally, to get rid of him, they gave Chris some ships and he set sail, and landed in the New World on Columbus Day, which was very convenient. If he had landed a month later, the Columbus Day Parade would interfere with the Thanksgiving Parade, which would be unfortunate.

So, Who's Dead These Days?

Some time ago an expert, in some kind of Malthusian snit about the increase in world population, wrote the statement that there are, at this moment, more people alive than there are dead.   He didn't explain how he arrived at that conclusion. Was he including all of the Neanderthal, Cro-Magnon and other largely fossilized folks of prehistory? Does he have a nose count of those early citizens? There were very few efficient census takers circulating among the caves in those days, and the cemetery records from the Neolithic Era probably aren't much to speak of, either.

It seems as though an awful lot of people are dead. Just about anybody I ever heard of is dead.

George Washington is dead. Attila the Hun is dead. Tom Mix is dead. Henry VIII is dead. Mata Hari is dead. Elvis Presley is more than likely dead. Name anybody who was born before the second Grover Cleveland administration, and chances are he or she is dead. For hundreds of thousands of years, they were just dropping like flies.

One of the hard things to remember as you move into late middle age, and your memory becomes erratic, is who's dead.

If the name of some remote person like Muhammad or Cleopatra or Ulysses S. Grant or Fannie Hurst comes up in conversation, you can be reasonably sure that person has passed on to his or her reward.

But more recent celebrities are hard to keep up with. The

name of some elderly entertainer or politician is mentioned, and the memory cells begin to churn. Did I read somewhere that this individual is no longer with us?

A related aspect of celebrity deadness is the occasional person that all sensible people know darn well is completely dead, but a small and vocal minority insists is secretly alive.

Elvis is the latest posthumous victim of this kind of mythology. Fanatic admirers decline to accept the mortality of their hero, and proclaim that he is living somewhere in the shadows.

The pathetic believers of these contemporary legends refuse to listen if told that this is a common phenomenon. When the late James Dean became late, back in 1955, many of his fans announced that he had survived the fatal auto crash and was hiding somewhere because he was lamentably disfigured.

In 1944, when orchestra leader Glenn Miller's airplane vanished over the English Channel, inconsolable teenage girls spoiled their families' Christmas by spending the holiday sobbing, "He's not really dead. They'll find him."

Rumors circulated that Miller had been seen in Paris, disfigured (a popular ingredient of this delusion), playing his mellow trombone in obscure jazz clubs.

It's surprising that John Lennon hasn't become the object of this type of rumor. He and his co-Beatles share the charismatic qualifications to generate a "He's really still alive but brain damaged and being cared for by old friends in Liverpool" story.

Rumors that a lot of dead people aren't really dead may have influenced the expert who claimed that more people are living today than are dead. He may have included Elvis and skewed his statistics.

The truth probably is that just about everybody who ever lived is dead. Present company excepted.

The Art of Child Manipulation

Today's adults, unlike past generations, are able to apply the help and advice of many authorities on the behavior and raising of children. In spite of all the available expert information, a surprising number of kids manage to grow up and become almost normal.

Hey, Kids! Let's Talk Creatively

Do modern parents really need professional advice on how to start a conversation with their kids? Does anybody join me in finding that depressing?

A book by Jane M. Healy, Ph.D, is titled, "Is Your Bed Still There When You Close the Door?... and Other Playful Ponderings: How to Have Creative and Intelligent Conversations with Your Kids." Another educator has written "101 Educational Conversations With Your Kindergartner-First Grader".

A book club's description of Dr. Healy's work says in part that "Victorian parents thought 'children should be seen and not heard.' Today, we know better. Educators and psychologists alike believe children should not only be heard, they should also be listened to and encouraged to participate in conversations. Talking builds flexible thinking and creative problem-solving..."

Pardon some dismay from someone who was heard and listened to as a kid, who later heard and listened to a couple of his own children, and who now is doing the same with some grandchildren.

As a post-Victorian kid, I was thoroughly heard, listened to and encouraged to participate in conversations. One major modern difference is that nobody encouraged me to participate in conversations about things that most rational adults had decided were none of my business.

Today, a grandpop can find himself in a pleasant chat with a four-year old about private body parts and functions, using the finest of clinical names.

We are talking here about body parts that my generation would never, ever, have mentioned around the house. Not even if one of them fell off and we required medical attention.

These were words and concepts to be discussed only with our peers, in the schoolyard at recess, with appropriate wisecracks and snickering. We suspected that our parents knew about such things, and maybe discussed them out of our earshot. But there was a line that wasn't to be crossed, except by somebody willing to risk the old "I'll wash your mouth out with soap" routine.

At least, Dr. Healy's book seems to offer alternatives to the kind of hearing and listening that tends to cause grandparents bemused embarrassment.

But "Is Your Bed Still There When You Close the Door?" is just the sort of philosophical opening line you'd expect from a Ph.D. My grandchildren would probably respond, "Oh, grandpop," with patient amusement, because they're used to silliness from aging relatives, and would go on playing "The Search for Red October" on the GameBoy as though nothing had happened.

Most parents would be more interested in the question, "Were all those toys, books, games and items of clothing still there on the floor when you closed the bedroom door, and if so, what are you going to do about it?" The expectation would be that the question would build some flexible thinking and creative problem solving, or else.

My parents and grandparents didn't have high school diplomas, much less Ph.D.s, but they never seemed to have trouble starting a conversation with me. I don't recall ever being asked my opinion of the status of an unobserved bed, but we did talk about current events, neighbors, movies, relatives, radio programs, books, comic strips, sports, my school, my parents' jobs, how things were when they were young — we didn't have time to cover it all. When I became a parent, the family also seemed always to be able to dredge up a conversational topic or two when called upon.

Maybe it was too practical. Maybe we all missed something by ignoring the metaphysics of the bed behind the closed door.

Social Growth at Playgrounds

A newspaper article about playgrounds advised parents on how to evaluate a playground before allowing their children to hang out in it. The advice didn't include things I'd already thought of, like checking whether the chains on the swings were rusted through or the sliding board led to an alligator pit.

The article suggested that parents should "think about whether this is a place your child will be emotionally secure and whether the equipment is developmentally appropriate and conducive to social growth."

An expert from Wellesley College warned that when evaluating a playground, "you have to think of the whole person, of the emotional and creative well-being."

Now, when you take the kids or grandkids to the playground, you'll worry every time they bellyflop down the sliding board or dangle by their heels from the monkey bars.

Not about broken bones. About whether what they're doing is developmentally appropriate.

Public playgrounds are a fairly recent adult intrusion on children's lives. As a city kid, back about the time that Joe Louis knocked out James J. Braddock for the heavyweight championship, I played mostly in the street, and I don't remember stumbling into any emotional insecurity that was more than momentary.

There was a blocks-long open lot nearby with a sandlot ball field, a good place to play when the street got boring. A few guys could toss a ball around the bases of the dusty infield on a sunbroiled summer afternoon, oblivious of any theories of experts from Wellesley.

When I was about seven, city officials started thinking about the whole person, and fenced in a piece of that lot, installed developmentally appropriate play equipment, and launched the neighborhood's first playground with adult supervision.

I went on opening day to try it out. I wasn't inside the fence 30 seconds when a kid built like a sumo wrestler walked up to me, leered nastily and punched me in the schnozzle.

The adult supervisor, alert to my emotional and creative well-being, came over immediately. She told me to hit the kid back.

I went home and read a book.

When I was 12, I was in a group that was sent once a week from our school to another school about a mile away for shop classes. We were dismissed early because of the long walk home.

Our route took us past a new municipal playground. It was fenced in and the gate was locked. We would climb over the fence and play on the equipment. Nearby residents would call the cops, who would come and chase us out of this facility that our parents paid for with their taxes, because it wasn't the time the city leaders had scheduled for us to do anything conducive to social growth on the swings.

Years later, when I was too old to care, that other big lot

with the dusty infield was fenced in and turned into an official, full-fledged Recreation Center, with designer playground equipment, a fancy post-sandlot ball diamond, a large brick building, an ice skating rink and the name of a local deceased politician.

I'm sure that the thoroughly-organized things the recreators allow kids to do there, when the gate isn't locked, are entirely developmentally appropriate and conducive to social growth.

But I suspect that tossing a ball around the infield was more fun.

Scholars at Work and Play

Scholar comes right after schnook in the dictionary, but let's not hold that against any scholars. Being an expert on things must be hard on the brain.

Computers Back the Bard

Scholars at a college in California made a complicated computerized study of the vocabulary, grammar and structure of plays by an uneducated former juvenile delinquent named William Shakespeare.

When they were finished, they made a startling announcement. Shakespeare's plays, the computers revealed, were written by Shakespeare.

For many years, an assortment of stuffy intellectuals have paraded through the literary world shouting that somebody else wrote Shakespeare's plays.

Among the nominees for the title of the real author are Sir Francis Bacon, the Earl of Oxford, Christopher Marlowe, Sir Walter Raleigh, Queen Elizabeth I, and just about every deceased writer but Fanny Hurst, Chic Sale, Dr. Seuss and Omar Khayyam.

The professors and pundits who want to jettison Shakespeare from the rolls of playwrights have come up with all sorts of arguments. Shakespeare could not have produced some of the greatest writing in the English language, they say, because:

His parents were illiterate.

He was uneducated.

He spelled his own name several different ways.

He liked to sue people, and was a greedy businessman.

He married an older woman because he got her pregnant.

He poached deer.

It's easy to see why prim, proper, pompous Ph.D's don't want to believe that Will Shakespeare could have turned out the premiere plays and poetry of our tongue. They have invested much time and money in acquiring academic degrees and intellectual reputations, and yet they know they couldn't have produced a "Hamlet" or a "Macbeth".

They don't want to believe that an average guy with no credentials could do what Will Shakespeare did.

They miss one point. An ordinary, uncouth, maybe even obnoxious guy can also, incidentally, be a genius.

And they carefully overlook other significant facts about Shakespeare's life. His father may have been illiterate, but he was a prosperous businessman and landlord in Stratford, and was elected mayor in 1568, when little Will was four. Not bad for somebody who couldn't read.

The Bard-to-be was 18 when he married a neighbor, Anne Hathaway, who was 26. Their first child was born six months later.

Will Shakespeare went to London (to avoid getting locked up for stealing deer from the land of the local member of Parliament, according to rumor) and in 1590 he started grinding out material for the stage, with lots of sex and violence.

It seems certain that he wrote his own plays, and pretty popular ones, because another playwright authored a pamphlet in 1592 attacking Shakespeare as an upstart who thought he was as good as university-trained writers.

In those days, the theater had about the same status that comic books do today. The stuffy literature experts have come a long way. Today they accept Shakespeare's plays as works of art.

Some day, the experts all may even agree that Shakespeare wrote them.

Voting to Decide What is True

A group of distinguished Biblical scholars got together and voted on which words in the New Testament they think Jesus really said, and which they think He almost said or might have said or never said. This is a democracy, after all, so things get decided by voting and the majority is always right.

Now that this concept is established, it will undoubtedly spread to lesser forms of scholarship.

Next, the Latin scholars will be voting on whether Caesar said all the stuff he says he said in "The Gallic Wars."

They will cast ballots to decide whether he really said that all Gaul is divided into three parts, or whether he said it was two parts or some other number of parts or no parts at all. Who knows? They may even vote that he wasn't talking about Gaul anyhow, but some other place.

Caesar wrote "The Gallic Wars" (I state confidently, since no scholars have voted against it yet that I know of) in 52 B.C. He would have had to be paying attention pretty hard to know that it was B.C., but it was.

He made all sorts of remarks about folks who, when they got around to it later, became the Germans and the Swiss and the Belgians and the French.

It may no longer be politically correct to quote Caesar as gossiping about the ancestors of our European allies. It must be time to convene a Caesar Seminar and let the scholars vote on what parts of the book were really Caesar's words, and what parts were produced by some sadistic Roman to make things unpleasant for 20th century school kids studying Latin.

The mathematics scholars will be next.

They'll assemble to vote on whether two plus two equals four, or some other number, or maybe doesn't equal anything at all.

After all, the first person to make the presumptuous statement that two plus two equals four was probably some primitive cave dweller who put two rocks next to two other rocks, and was edified to notice that there were four of them under those circumstances.

At our advanced stage of civilization, we can't take the word of some scraggly bison-hunter about serious subjects. Scholars should vote on this as soon as possible.

And can we go on airily accepting the pronouncement of Sir Isaac Newton, who wore a black robe and a funny wig and forgot to duck when apples fell on him, that every action has an equal and opposite reaction? When are the physicists going to vote and settle this?

Here's a final idea, if we are going to start using the ballot box in the scholarship field.

All of those Bible scholars who voted on the Jesus quotes in the New Testament, if they teach classes, should let their students vote on whether or not to accept the words of the text books, or the words in the teacher's lectures.

No. That might not work. The students aren't experts yet. After they get their degrees in a subject, then they'll be qualified to vote that the truths they just learned aren't true.

Baby Talk and Old Grouches

Results of two scholarly studies were reported on the same day. One study revealed that mothers can improve their children's vocabularies by talking to them more. The other determined that older men get cranky faster than older women.

This is really exciting information.

Who would have dreamed that kids learn more words if they hear more words? Aren't you glad that some highly educated experts spent a lot of time and money delving into this mystery? This calls for a follow-up study, which might discover that kids learn to talk in the first place by hearing other people talk.

The survey results have deep significance for mothers. It proves that if they don't want their kids talking all the time, they shouldn't talk to them so much.

The brief news report about the survey didn't go into details. It didn't say, for instance, whether the vocabulary increase only works when the mother does the extra talking.

Does it work when the father talks more to the kid? Or Uncle Earl? Or the woman next door?

And what kind of new words does a child learn from these increased conversations? Should the mother just chatter away about things that interest her, and produce a prodigy sitting in the high chair saying, "chain stitch" and "credit card" and "go to the mall" and "bingo night" and "let's eat out"?

If the father does the extra talking, you might have a kid with increased word power lolling in the playpen chattering, "earned run average" and "four-wheel drive" and "union dues" and "what's for dinner" and other masculine concepts.

Maybe the survey is more astonishing than it seems. Maybe this vocabulary-building works in some arcane manner that has nothing to do with what the mother says, but gets the baby using new words regardless of the mother's input.

Maybe the mother says, "See the pussycat?" and the child replies, "Yes, I observe the feline." And the mother says "Eat your strained beans" and the baby coos, "Very well, I shall consume my legume puree." If that's the way the vocabulary building works, it's worth a scientific study.

Otherwise, the whole study sounds like a waste of time to me. But maybe I'm just becoming a grouchy old man.

The reason men become grouches faster than women become grouchettes, according to that other scientific study, is that the brain cells that control grouchiness deteriorate first in men.

My own observation is that it's the brain cells that remember people's names that are the first to go.

I haven't noticed myself getting grouchy as I get older. What I have noticed is that there's a lot more to complain about these days than there used to be.

Watching TV from a Distance

The first observation in this chapter was written just after a TV network newscast was enduring some criticism. The second was done during the 1992 presidential campaign. Any television watcher who has noticed vast improvements since then, please give me a buzz.

All the News That's Fit to Invent

It has been at least several days since one of the network television news operations got caught inventing news.

In case you missed it because you were watching "Married With Children" reruns instead of news broadcasting (Al Bundy and the world news are just about equally depressing), a television network admitted fabricating some news pictures recently.

In a report that claimed a certain brand of truck occasionally blew up when in a collision, news producers rigged a truck with explosives. They wanted to make sure it wouldn't remain unexploded when they filmed a staged collision, and thus disappoint the information-hungry viewers.

The network executives were hardly finished apologizing for that incident when the same news organization did a report about environmental problems killing fish in a western river. The reporters were discovered to have shown films of unrelated dead fish in a different river, as well as other fish they told the audience were dead, but were actually just taking a nap.

A network apologist didn't seem to think the problems were a big deal. Newspapers often run corrections, she said.

But corrections of newspaper articles usually point out a wrong fact that crept into print because of carelessness, stupidity, or some supposedly reliable source providing incorrect information.

When was the last time you saw a newspaper correction like this: "The report in yesterday's Daily Flugelhorn that certain trucks explode in accidents neglected to mention that our reporters blew up a truck themselves in a fake accident in order to describe the problem."

Television people probably have been watching too much television. The difference between the Nightly News and the Movie of the Week may be getting blurred.

Vehicles get spectacularly blown up routinely on dramatic programs that are fiction. We all know what great fun that is to watch. The news people may feel that they're not doing their job if real life isn't as exciting as "Matlock", so they're tempted to throw in some entertaining enhancements.

One network spokesperson, in discussing the situation, said something about "responsible journalism."

Hold on, there. Custom, dictionaries and other frequently ignored authorities indicate that journalists are persons who write for newspapers or magazines. The folks on television are broadcasters, not journalists. They include themselves in "the press," but they aren't the press. They're the transmitter.

The nature of their business means that broadcasters have to go to elaborate lengths to make up stories. Broadcasters have to wire explosives under a truck to be sure it will explode when they want to film a truck explosion.

Journalists are lucky. All we would have to do is peck out on the keyboard, "The truck exploded with a mighty roar.

Flames engulfed the chassis in seconds."

We could do it without cameras, without explosives, without trucks, without even leaving the office. We're less tempted to do it, because we aren't part of an entertainment medium like the TV newsies.

Most people still trust journalists to describe reality. Most people trust television broadcasters to photograph reality. But surveys in recent years reveal that the public's trust in news gatherers is gradually declining.

After that network's performances with the truck and the fish, it's no wonder.

Eight Seconds To Say It All

Folks who watch what passes for news coverage on television have been worked up about the so-called sound bite.

A sound bite is the tiny sliver of time usually allowed for an important person to make an important statement on television.

The major function of the sound bite is to allow time for a quick breath to be taken by the people who do most of the talking, the news readers whose only importance is that they have nice faces, nice voices and nice big salaries.

A couple of weeks ago, one major network announced that it was going to allow presidential candidates longer sound bites. They were going to be allowed to talk for 30 seconds at a chance.

Why, with that extravagant time allowance, candidates for the highest office in the land will be permitted to take up as much television time as the shortest toothpaste commercial.

The justice in that is obvious. If you had to choose, which could you get along without? Politicians, or teeth?

The news chief of that generous network was quoted as

admitting that "the average sound bite on the evening news runs from eight to 20 seconds."

If television had been with us through history, imagine how the eight-second sound bite would have handled famous speakers.

(Commentator): "At the Gettysburg Cemetery dedication today, the president said:"

(Start of eight-second sound bite): "Four score and seven years ago, our fathers brought forth on this continent a new nation, conceived in liberty and dedicated to the proposition."

(Commentator): "And in other news..."

In fairness, people have always liked short, snappy quotations. Before television started nibbling on the sound of people's statements, Americans tended to make heroes out of people who said things like, "My only regret is that I have but one life to give for my country" (four seconds) or "Don't give up the ship" (two seconds.)

Patrick Henry made a vehement, long winded speech, and all most of us know is the three second sound bite: "Give me liberty, or give me death."

But celebrities have suffered with the chopping off of their remarks in the pre-television-news days B. C. (before Cronkite.)

William Henry Vanderbilt, who was a millionaire by trade and made $1,200 an hour on his investments back in the 1880s, cancelled a train on a railroad he owned because it didn't have enough paying passengers to support it. A reporter suggested he should "run it for the public benefit."

"The public be damned," said Vanderbilt. "I am working for my stockholders. If the public want the train, why don't they pay for it?"

This seems like a reasonable attitude, one that most of us might share if we happened to own any railroads.

But sound bite-osis set in. All anybody ever quotes is Vanderbilt saying, "The public be damned."

This column, if it were emerging from the million dollar vocal cords of a network news reader, would last about two and a half minutes. That's the equivalent of 18 of those eight second sound bites.

Columnists aren't limited to bites. I can write a whole snack.

Warning: Sex And Violence

(The following newspaper column contains mentions of violence and sex. Reader discretion is advised.)

These weekly columns, though you may not have noticed it, rarely contain material of a violent nature. Nor do they often include sexual content, unless you are one of those readers easily turned on by an occasional incorrect pronoun reference.

It has been a long-unused policy that if I detected in advance that any violence or sex was going to creep into a column, I would warn you right up front, so you could switch to reading something less likely to offend you, like the Franklin, Indiana, phone book or the instructions for assembling a small utility building.

The television networks should be commended for following the lead of this column.

Networks now are making little warning announcements at the start of programs, and also in promotions of upcoming shows. They scrupulously let us know when they intend to depict people engaging in violent behavior, removing too many garments or enjoying physical activities that might upset the more conservative members of groups like the Girl Scouts of America, the International Edsel Club, the Colonial Dames of XVII Century or the Two-Seeds-in-the-Spirit Predestinarian Baptists.

The broadcasters were encouraged to provide such warnings of potential turpitude by worried government operatives, who have been pondering the problem almost since that glorious day when fun-loving television producers first discovered the entertainment value of depictions of murder, rape, car crashes, incest and aggravated assault.

This policy of announcing that undesirable material is forthcoming could cause problems.

The simultaneous rush of millions of viewers all over the nation, dashing across living rooms to change the channel before they are compelled to witness something like a decapitation or a disrobing, could set up vibrations that might disrupt the balance of the continent's tectonic plates and cause severe earth tremors. (Play it safe. Use your remote.)

But we must be prepared to take small risks for the great value of being told when something overstimulating might appear on the tube.

A pioneer in this sort of thing was Mickey Spillane, the mystery writer. In his early novels, about 40 years ago, he thoughtfully used italic type to emphasize sections in which female characters removed their clothing (which they did with astonishing frequency) and attempted to lure the hero into disreputable situations.

This generous gesture by the writer allowed readers to skip over the disturbing parts of the book, and to concentrate on the unfolding detective story without their morals being impaired.

There are wrong thinkers among us who believe that brother Spillane could simply have left out the detailed descriptions of feminine garment removal and other lurid (and italicized) behavior. The same folks probably think that the television networks could omit the sex and violence from their entertainments.

Such critics suggest the possibility that there may be people who actually like to watch this stuff. Why, some people might even be encouraged to tune in to a program by the very announcements designed to warn them away.

Nah. The television people wouldn't think of anything like that.

18,000 Murders? That's Show Biz

A national newsletter reported that the average American child sees 18,000 murders on television before he or she graduates from high school.

Can that be true? Assume 15 years of TV watching, at 365 days each plus three Leap Days, times six hours a day. To see the allotted 18,000 murders, a kid would have to catch one killing every hour and 49 minutes.

It could be done. But it would take dedication, concentration and coordination, with the remote control in one hand and TV Guide in the other.

Even so, pronouncements of this type induce worriers to believe that seeing violence on television encourages violent behavior among the viewers. It's not clear exactly when the TV-influenced kids have time to go out and assault somebody, if they spend all that time in front of the TV set.

Television industry leaders loudly deny that seeing behavior on television can motivate a person to emulate it. Except, of course, when the industry representatives are talking to folks who spend big bucks on advertising; then they insist that showing a brand of beer being guzzled or a make of auto being driven will send the watching consumers out, zombie-like, to do likewise.

The entertainment media have always been picked on for depicting too much sex and violence. Any new medium that emerged, be it movies, radio, comic books, theater, strolling minstrels or possibly even paleolithic cave drawings, has been cited as stimulating violence.

The prevailing opinion says that parents need to protect their children from these sordid influences. That means that today's parents also have to give up the pleasure of watching televised mayhem, which is often a family activity.

Back in the days when TV was still a gleam in Vladimir Zworykin's iconoscope, my father drove some distance to take me to see a British film called "The Demon Barber of Fleet Street." We shared delighted laughter as the razor-wielding barber slit the gullets of innocent customers and turned the corpses over to the woman in the pie shop next door to be ground up and baked in tasty casseroles.

But my father was anxious to protect me. In the same era, he forbade me to listen to a radio series called "Chandu the Magician." I have no idea why, because I never heard the program, but at age nine I used to shiver at the thought that Chandu must have done worse things than the Demon Barber (who later became Sweeney Todd and sang while he worked.)

Can children be sheltered from exposure to violence? We should start by forbidding them to watch television news broadcasts, or to read the newspaper.

And keep the kid out of the library. It's terrifying what an innocent child might be exposed to there.

For example: when I was in junior high school, I came across the story of two brothers who rape a woman and cut off her hands and tongue, so she can't tell or write the attackers' names. There are three murders before that happens, but there isn't space for the complicated but dull details here.

The rape victim's brothers are framed for two of the earlier murders, but the emperor tells their father that the sons won't be executed if the father cuts off his own hand. The father ships his hand to the emperor, who executes the sons anyway and sends the hand and the sons' heads back by return mail.

The raped girl uses a stick in her mouth to write her attackers' names in sand. They happen to be the empress's sons. For revenge, the victim's father kills the rapists (single-handed, literally), grinds them up in meat pies, and invites their mother over for dinner. When she's done the meal, he reveals the recipe, and practically everybody who's still in one piece

stabs everybody else dead. (There is also a racist subplot.)
Do you want your kids reading stuff like that?

Don't worry. The author of that mind-warping piece of trash was William Shakespeare. And any English teacher will tell you that your typical American school kids will go to extraordinary lengths to avoid reading anything by Shakespeare. If the students thought it was by Stephen King, they'd probably go for it.

Animal Stories

There is an old and durable opinion that animal stories interest a whole bunch of your average readers. The opinion probably refers to tales about puppies and kitty cats and other beasts that emanate cuteness. I'm not sure where poisonous birds fit in, or dogs that say "gong-gong", or eastern narrow mouth toads. But that seems to be what we have here. Any reader who demands cuteness will have to look elsewhere.

Species Come, Species Go

All admirers of creepy eight-legged creatures were edified to hear reports from Cambridge, England, about the discovery of a previously unknown species of spider.

It's doubtful that anyone really needed another kind of spider. There seem to be enough sorts of spiders to please the fussiest person. But like it or not, a new type of spider has been found.

If the reports coming out of Cambridge don't contain a misplaced decimal point, this new make and model of spider measures only four one-hundredths of an inch across the beam. That may explain why nobody has stumbled over one before.

A layperson would think that anyone looking for a spider of this size would start the search by peering up water spouts. It is a well-known scientific fact that eensy-weensy spiders frequent water spouts. (Another school of thought has it that the spiders who go up water spouts are of the inky-dinky variety, but let's not get too entomologically technical here.)

It's no surprise that Cambridge was the place that this highly miniaturized spider was discovered. The university there is full of folks who sit around all day contemplating subatomic particles, so it's no wonder that it was a Cambridgean (Cambridgite? Cambridger?) who noticed the existence of a bug that small.

And it's pleasant to hear of a new species being announced. These days we are told mostly of species that are disappearing.

It seems that the endangered species are always things we would miss of they extincted themselves, like whales, whooping cranes, Bengal tigers or rhinoceroses. Nothing ever seems to endanger beasts we could do without, like sewer rats, garden slugs, termites or mosquitoes.

Not that it wouldn't be annoying if a rhinoceros or tiger found its way into the carport and messed around with the trash can some night. And a whale in the marigold bed would probably be somewhat disruptive.

But those are only occasional problems. Mosquitoes are with us always, eager to puncture our epidermis at every opportunity.

A few of the more popular animal species are endangered because human beings want to make selfish use of some chunk of them or other. The rhinoceros population is being reduced because wealthy but insecure Oriental gentlemen believe that ingesting ground-up rhino horn is beneficial to their sex life.

As a public service, maybe some competent international public relations firm could start a subtle campaign to convince our Far Eastern brethren that pulverized mosquito carcasses make a strong aphrodisiac.

Asians would then start buying up mosquitoes by the kilo. Adventurous entrepreneurs would organize profitable mosquito roundups. Mosquito-meat auctions would produce spectacular prices. Mosquito poachers would be everywhere.

Soon, mosquitoes would go on the endangered species list, recognition they richly and famously deserve, and dinner on the patio would be rescued as an American institution.

Naturally, the impending extinction of the mosquito would stir up some environmental do-gooders into forming a "Save the Mosquitoes" campaign. But they wouldn't have a chance. The bug-bite scratchers of the world would have them outnumbered.

A New Worry: Poisonous Birds

The relentless quest for human knowledge took another oblique lunge when scientists announced the discovery of the first known poisonous bird.

The first reports induced tentative visions of a mean-looking, vulturesque fowl that would swoop down, emitting fearsome screams, and attack its terrified victim with a venom-injecting peck.

Nope. This critter, its discoverers report, is a mild-mannered little orange-and-black songbird.

If you want to get poisoned by it, you have to lick it.

After a conscientious, though brief, attempt to remember the last time I applied my tongue to any of our feathered friends, I decided that I'm probably safe from poisoning by this bird.

The bird was discovered loitering around the jungles of New Guinea, where it has eluded the attention of the rest of the world. A songbird that chooses to hang out in New Guinea is as unlikely to get any recognition as a cricket player in Omaha or a furnace repairman in Nigeria.

The local folks in the jungle call the bird pitohui, pronounced PIT-a-hooey, and you can see how it got its name. Pit-a-hooey is precisely what I would say after I licked a bird, poisonous or not.

Why, I sense you asking, would anybody in his or her right

mind lick a bird, even in the jungles of New Guinea where there is probably not much else to do to while away the hours?

Well, it seems that a jungle expedition was trapping birds in nets, for some ornithological project (or maybe just for unmotivated orneriness; who knows?) and one of the trappers cut his hand after touching a pitooey-bird. He licked the cut on his hand, and his mouth turned numb.

After thinking it over, and realizing he hadn't been in contact with any poison ivy, novocaine or adversarial fists recently, the numb-lipped scientist began to suspect that the innocent-looking orange-and-black songbird was responsible for his fat lip.

The next time they caught one of the birds, he and his fellow researchers licked it. A minute or two later, they were all standing around with numb lips, saying to each other, "See at? It uz the ird atter all. We etter det dis ird ack to the laratory."

Laboratory analysis revealed that the pitohui's feathers and skin are full of something called homobatrachotoxin, probably another of those exotic native words from the New Guinea jungle.

An extract of pitohui-bird juice was whipped up in the blender down at the lab, and the researchers found that 10 milligrams of essence of pitohui killed a mouse in less than 20 minutes.

If my recollection of the metric system is not too fuzzy, milligrams come about a half million to the pound, and therefore 10 of the little suckers isn't much poison, even for mice. So even those of us who are somewhat bigger than mice had better cancel any plans we had for pitohui-licking.

Just what we needed. Something else to worry about. Something else to remember.

Now, whenever we happen to be passing through the New Guinea jungle on the way over to K-Mart, we will have to keep saying to ourselves, over and over, "Don't lick any birds. Don't lick any birds. Don't lick any birds."

The Case of the Toad by the Road

Here's instructive news for any citizens who are fighting against some intrusive project like a new eight-lane highway that will pass through the impatiens bed in your side yard, or a housing development planned in the meadow across the street, or a landfill proposed next to the neighborhood playground. You can put a halt to the situation by applying the newly discovered toad-by-the-road method.

A road-widening project in southern Maryland has been blocked because an endangered species might be affected, even though nobody has seen any dues-paying members of the species hanging around there since 1986.

The road-altering department of St. Mary's County wants to widen one of the local roads. But the $2.3 million project is stopped dead.

The county asked the state for permission. The official state species protectors dug into the files, and found that an eastern narrow-mouthed toad had been seen loitering in the neighborhood back in '86.

The species has been on the Maryland endangered species list since 1972. That bans insensitive road-wideners from possibly extending their widenings into any puddle that the eastern narrow-mouthed toad might need to keep itself unendangered.

The toad experts maintain that even though no other endangered toads have been noticed lolling about St. Mary's County for all these years, that doesn't mean they aren't there.

Those among us who are not toad experts might be so unscientific as to suggest that the same logic could be applied to any endangered species.

Among the loyal representatives of endangered species that have not been noticed in St. Mary's County, Md., recently are the southeastern beach mouse, the black rhinoceros, the Ozark big-eared bat, the wild yak, the Chinese river dolphin and

Attwater's greater prairie chicken.

But, according to the reasoning applied to the protection of the eastern narrow-mouthed toad, the absence of any or all of these critters, and many others, doesn't mean they aren't there.

The reupholstering of the road remains on hold while the experts on how wide a road should be negotiate with the experts on how protected a toad should be.

This case comes as great news for anyone looking to frustrate bureaucrats who are trying to dump a huge load of progress all over a neighborhood.

Tell them they can't build, widen, tear down, rezone or otherwise depredate whatever piece of nearby turf they plan to attack, because an endangered species might be frolicking there.

Tell them you saw a prime but endangered specimen of Bachman's wood warbler preening its feathers in the weeds on the site. Tell them that an endangered asian wild ass (equus hemianmus) was noticed grazing on some endangered ranunculus acriformis just down the hill a ways.

If the officials give you an argument, refer them to the Maryland toad situation; tell them that bone fide environmental authorities insist that just because you don't see an endangered species in the vicinity doesn't mean it isn't there.

This should bring the oncoming procession of backhoes, front end loaders and guys with hard hats to a sudden halt. Won't that be fun?

Can a Vehicle Have Four Legs?

A fellow down in Pike County, Kentucky, is fighting a charge of operating a vehicle while intoxicated.

What he was operating while intoxicated was a horse.

The Kentuckian maintains that a horse is not a vehicle. "She's got a mind of her own," he says of his horse, Mable. "I don't think a vehicle has a mind."

Indeed, he says, he has often gone home astride Mable after imbibing too much at local drinking establishments, and always got there safely because Mable, unlike your average motor vehicle, operates automatically.

"I've even passed out in the saddle before," the accused rider reports. "She knows the way home."

It would seem that, if there are folks who feel compelled to drink and drive, it is better for society if they drive a four-legged, self-directed vehicle that doesn't have to be steered or braked.

I've seen the system in action. When I was a small boy, in the dim days beyond recall, the man who lived next door to our house was a huckster. He traveled the streets in a horse-drawn wagon, selling vegetables and fruit.

On Monday through Thursday, he arrived home around sundown in a normal and respectable fashion, driving the two horses up to his gates and then leading them into the wagon yard.

Fridays were different. The horses would come clopping along the street, pull up outside the wooden fence and wait patiently for a family member to open up the gates and let them in. The driver, if he could be called that on those occasions, would be lolling on the wagon seat, snoozing peacefully.

Maybe I misjudged the situation. Maybe he was just exhausted from the week's commercial travail. But it was my childhood impression that on Fridays, he stopped off at some refreshment purveyor's on the way home and consumed excessive quantities of hearty liquids.

And the horses knew the way home. I don't know how far they had to come, but they traveled the city streets weekly without known incident and got their owner back to his family safely. If he had been at the wheel of a motor truck, it would probably have concluded most Fridays mashed against a pole somewhere.

These memories lead me to sympathize with the inebriated horseman in Kentucky. It seems to me that a horse is only a vehicle when its driver is telling it what to do. If the person in the saddle in semiconscious, due to injudicious imbibing, and the horse is proceeding on its own recognizance, the person can hardly be awarded credit or blame for anything that happens, and the horse should be commended for showing more responsibility than the rider.

Some of the facts in the Kentucky case confuse the issue a bit. When a Kentucky state trooper (who was in an automobile, unquestionably a vehicle) started to pursue the under-the-influence equestrian, Mable galloped away, ran headlong into a tree and fell on top of her rider.

If this was the result of the rider's faulty navigation, than he probably was a drunken driver, Mable did at the moment qualify as a vehicle, and the guy has lost his argument.

On the other hand, if Mable acted on her own accord, the "mind of her own" that her owner brags about was not making the best decisions under the circumstances.

Did anybody give Mable a Breathalizer test?

A New Way to Bag the Limit

The state of Michigan has improved its game laws by making it legal for people with hunting licenses to pick up dead animals they find lying along the road, and count them toward their season hunting limit.

This is good news for that great legion of hunters who often spend hours and days tramping resolutely through the woods, displaying a large certificate that says they are entitled to blast the first deer that wanders into their range of vision, and come home without experiencing so much as a fleeting glimpse of a flicking white tail in the bushes.

There's always a chance that a local kid in a pickup truck

might wallop a deer out on the highway.

The hapless, deerless hunter who is driving home with no carcass draped on his roof rack may be lucky enough to come upon the deceased deer along the roadside while the truck driver, with no license to scoop up the mangled venison, is out conferring with a body shop about the mess the collision made of his truck's right front.

Some hunters might be a little embarrassed to bring home a deer that was dispatched by a motor vehicle. No matter what the hunting license allows, most hunters are looking for bragging rights to go along with the possibilities of taxidermy or venisonburgers.

But a hunter with high creativity and low scruples could always back off a ways and put a bullet into an appropriately fatal area of the already expired deer. That evidence, plus an imaginative but plausible tale of cunning woodsmanship and precise marksmanship, should keep up the hunter's reputation with the home folks.

That wouldn't work so well with rabbits. A slightly flattened trophy would arouse suspicion, especially one with tread marks.

There are some other temptations built into this Michigan game policy. For every bumper sticker that says, "I brake for animals," there may now be a driver who guns the engine when he sees a rabbit, pheasant or turkey crossing the highway in front of him. If he can successfully smack a potential dinner with his car, his hunting license says he can keep it.

Fortunately for all the Michigan deer, the new policy probably won't encourage deer hunting by vehicle. You can buy venison cheaper than the cost of the damage usually done when a deer and a car collide at full speed.

But foxes and raccoons had better watch out. They're valuable. The son of a friend of mine used to make a lot of money by picking up mashed animals he spotted along the road and selling the pelts to the same people who buy furs from trappers. And he didn't even have a hunting license.

One thing the reports from Michigan don't make clear: If you have a fishing license, does that mean that any fish you run over, you can keep?

What Does the Doggie Say?

Harper's magazine published a list of what dogs say in other countries. The words people use to imitate the sound of barking were compiled by Frost & Sullivan, a market research firm, to help dog food companies with overseas advertising.

Every right-thinking American knows that doggies say bow-wow, or, if being more formal, woof-woof. This is one of the first lessons conveyed to each of us while we are still in our mother's arms or thereabouts. Is there a person anywhere in the land who was never asked, during his or her formative years, "What does the doggie say?"

But less enlightened folks in foreign lands seem to hear canine emissions differently.

Or maybe dogs of other countries actually make different sounds.

The list tells us that dogs in our linguistic motherland, the United Kingdom, say woof-woof. This was to be expected. There was probably once a time when the sun never set on woof.

In Germany, says the report, dogs say wuff-wuff. That sounds familiar, although there is the suspicion that a German dog might pronounce it vuff-vuff.

Danish dogs, we are told, do say vuf-vuf. And in the Netherlands, barking is transcribed as woef-woef, which is probably just good old fashioned woofing. We can't expect dogs to be consistent spellers.

And dogs in Luxembourg say wau-wau. That's such a small country that dogs don't need full-scale woofs to be heard there.

An American ear can even handle some of the stranger European variations, like the sound of Czechoslovakian dogs (if they haven't all been redesignated as either Czech dogs or Slovak dogs) barking haf-haf.

It's possible to accept Spanish dogs saying guau-guau, apparently pronounced hwow-hwow. (Although in the Catalonian part of Spain, we are led to believe, the dogs say bup-bup.)

And we can stretch a bit and accept Italian dogs barking bau-bau, Finnish dogs saying hau-hau, or Estonian dogs saying auh-auh.

But when the report begins to transliterate barking from some of the more geographically remote dogs, the English-hearing mind can't avoid some incredulity.

For example: Romanian dogs are reported to say ham-ham. Portuguese observers believe their dogs say ao-ao, and the letter A has a little horizontal line over it. Come on, now; no dog knows how to put a diacritical mark on top of his bark.

Even worse: in Indonesia, according to the published list, people think their dogs say gong-gong. In Laos, it's voon-voon. In the Philippines, it's aw-aw. In Taiwan, it's wang-wang. In Thailand, it's hong-hong.

There is a distinct suspicion here that our leg is being pulled, with the force of a Great Dane yanking on the ankle.

Can there really be a dog anywhere in the world that makes a noise that sounds like gong-gong? A dogfight in Indonesia must sound like a carillon collapsing.

Well, let us hope that this research into phonetic barking helps American dog food manufacturers create advertising that attracts lots of international business. It would be too bad if they are voon-vooning up the wrong tree.

A Real Cat and Dog Fight

The City Council in Pittsburgh had the temerity to propose that cats be licensed, and the cat lovers there set up a terrible howl.

The fact that dog licenses have long been an accepted part of American life and culture did not impress the Pittsburgh cat owners. They are ready to demand a Constitutional amendment creating a separation of feline and state, and guaranteeing equal treatment under the law regardless of species (except dogs.)

Now, Pittsburgh is a peculiar place by the standards of Philadelphia, which is the part of the universe I normally frequent. Out there on the slopes of the Alleghenies, waitresses ask you, "What'll yins have?" instead of "What'll yiz have?" as they do here; a person who wants to buy a hot dog and a soda has to ask for a weeny and a pop, and phrases like "The grass needs cut" or "The car needs washed" are considered acceptable grammatical construction.

Furthermore, Pittsburgh is the only major burg in the country that the Postal Service hasn't convinced to drop the "h" from its end. So some odd behavior there may be expected.

But when it comes to massive resistance to cat licensing, Pittsburgh may not be that unique. Cat fanciers in any area tend to be defensive, if not belligerent, on the subject of feline rights.

Dog owners have placidly accepted licencing through the years. The different attitudes of dog people and cat people reflect an understanding of the differences between cats and dogs.

If animals drove cars, dogs would wear seat belts and cats wouldn't. For exercise, dogs would go for a stroll and cats would do aerobics. Dogs would play golf and cats would bungee-jump.

In a restaurant, dogs would order steak and cats would order filet of sole. Dogs would play bridge and cats would play poker. Dogs would read the New York Times and cats would read the Daily News.

Dogs would smoke pipes and cats would smoke cigarettes. Dogs would listen to Sinatra and cats would listen to the Rolling Stones. Dogs would buy certificates of deposit and cats would play the stock market. Dogs would drink beer and cats would drink white wine.

And dogs, as good citizens, are willing to wear a license dangling from their collars. Cats resist even the collars.

Cats get away with plenty. They wander more freely than dogs, and draw fewer complaints when they do anti-social things in neighbors' yards. And their owners stick up for them.

Why cats have earned special privileges over dogs, I don't know. But there is one good reason why municipalities have resisted cat licensing. With dog licenses there follows the inevitability of the dog catcher.

No rational person would want the job of municipal cat catcher.

Cats are virtually uncatchable. When they do get caught, they are inclined to thrash around, yowl, squirm, screech, contort, hiss, wriggle, scratch, bite and make an embarrassing scene.

Rounding up unlicensed cats is a job feasible only for Marine Corps veterans, professional wrestlers, retired kindergarten teachers and others experienced in subduing the unruly.

A suggestion: Pittsburgh cat licenses should be made of steel and each should weigh 75 pounds. That might help revive the steel industry, and would certainly keep the cats from straying.

Some Bank Accounts

Banking as we know it dates to the founding of the Bank of Amsterdam in 1609. Before that, people had to apply to wealthy private individuals if they wanted to be told they couldn't borrow any money.

Poor Robbery Writing Skills

Bank robbers tend to have a peculiarity that is puzzling. They like to communicate by handing bank tellers pieces of paper. The idea of paperwork as a banking necessity has sunk into their little minds. Rarely does a bank robber make a verbal demand. He usually hands the bank employee a note.

Since they seem to be committed to the idea of written communication, you'd think they would be better at it.

One would-be robber a few years ago handed a note to a teller in a Philadelphia bank. She studied the document and shoved it back to him.

"What does this say?" she demanded angrily. "I can't read this."

The robber, rattled, took back his note and left. Here we had, presumably, two products of the public schools; he couldn't write clearly and she couldn't read well, and it prevented a robbery.

On another occasion, a man walked up to a startled employee in the Federal Reserve Bank of Philadelphia and handed over a note demanding money.

The Fed employee explained patiently that, while a function of the Federal Reserve is to distribute money to the area's banks, there was no cash available to hand out to the average robber off the street.

The ill-informed robber said he was sorry. And he asked if he could please have his note back.

There was one incident in which a robber wrote his demand for money on a deposit slip, which he dutifully filled in, including his account number. He did, indeed, have an account at the bank, and the grateful police found it rather easy to track him down.

In another cop-pleaser, a robber left behind his note, written on the back of his telephone bill.

Then, there was the unfortunate robber who did make a verbal demand. The teller told him that she was sorry, but it was against the bank rules to give a robber any money if he didn't have a note. The guy left empty handed.

Another pathetic failure was the case of a robber who handed a teller a note demanding that she put money in a paper bag.

"Where's the bag?" asked the teller.

"I don't have one," said the robber.

"Well, neither do I," said the teller with an exasperated tone. The robber left.

To be fair to the bank robbers of the community, all of the odd behavior doesn't take place on the customer side of the counter. There was an instance in which a robber thrust the traditional note at a teller, and she activated a silent alarm. One of the bank's security troops immediately emerged from his back room command post.

"Which one of you girls is setting off the alarm?" he asked loudly. Even a bank robber with poor note-writing skills is smart enough to leave when he hears that.

Bank Defrauders
Need a Little Imagination

Three people in New York were nabbed by the FBI because they tried to cash a stolen check for $932,203 that was from the Canadian government and was made out to the United Nations Environmental Program Multilateral Ozone Fund.

Each of the culprits tried to deposit the check in his bank account, but they all found it hard to convince the tellers that they were acting on behalf of UNEPMOF. (I don't know for a fact that the United Nations Environmental Program Multilateral Ozone Fund calls itself UNEPMOF, but all international acronym-fanciers would agree that the odds favor it.)

The three unsuccessful fraud perpetrators obviously don't know much about banks.

It's hard enough to prove to most bank tellers that you are who you really are, much less trying to convince them that you're an entire United Nations agency.

Many years ago I dealt with a small town bank. The folks who worked there all knew me. Every Friday evening, when I stepped up to any teller window to cash my paycheck, the teller would say, "Hi, Jim."

Then a big city financial institution bought that bank. The next Friday when I went in, the teller said, "Hi, Jim. Do you have any identification?"

Some people get annoyed when banks demand identification. The same people would be furious if the bank didn't verify identification and some disreputable citizen got away with representing himself as them and made off with a big withdrawal from their account.

The New Yorkers who tried to cash the United Nations check didn't have as much imagination as a fellow who worked for a real estate office in White Plains, New York, in 1984.

This realty operative, obviously a few lots short of a subdivision when it came to financial maneuvers, noticed that nice big checks passed through his employer's establishment made out to banks.

He latched onto a check for $51,469 made out to Mellon Bank. He strolled down to a nearby small local bank and used the check as a deposit to open an account. He filled out the proper forms, writing down that his name was Mr. Mellon E. Bank.

The bank teller took his deposit. But a few days later, when Mr. Bank dropped in again and tried to withdraw $3,850 cash, the teller awoke from her fiduciary slumber and called the feds.

The FBI galloped to the scene and took Mr. M. E. Bank into custody. But even though he failed, the man had given it a good try.

The thieves with the UNEPMOF check might have had a little class and sent one of their group into a bank to open an account under the name of Mr. Unep Mof. With a name like that, he could represent himself as being from just about any Third World country, and give an address in a town on the Malay peninsula or near Lake Tanganyika.

If stuck with the full organization name on the check, he could have started a small business account as sole proprietor of the United Nations Environmental Program Multilateral Ozone Fund Termite Inspection Service.

He would still find himself socializing with several FBI special agents sooner or later, but at least the gang down at the U.S. Attorney's Office would forever smile when they thought of him.

The Sport of
Bureaucrat-Watching

Bureaucracies are like rhinoceroses. They are fun to watch from a distance, but they are large, clumsy and short-sighted, and when you have to deal with one close up, it usually runs right over you.

A Controversial Job Opportunity

The New Jersey Department of Education ran a help wanted advertisement for a "Director of Controversies and Disputes." That sounds like a good idea. Most controversies and disputes aren't very well organized and tend to bounce all over the place. They could use a little direction.

Controversies and disputes are quite common in New Jersey, and it's encouraging to see the state government trying to do something about them before they get out of hand.

The ad suggested that the applicant should have a doctorate either in education or in law. The hirers in Trenton would be advised to go with a lawyer. An educator's experience with controversies and disputes would most likely be with some uppity student who came stomping up to the desk after class and snarled, "What do you mean, giving me a C for this paper?"

A lawyer, on the other hand, probably had all of his or her controversies and disputes with other lawyers, a breed of human beings who have made controversing and disputing an esoteric blend of art and skill like sculpture, haiku poetry or Elvis impersonation. A typical lawyer would be ready, if not eager, to start directing every dispute that got slid through the mail slot.

That might even be a problem. Anybody qualified as Director of Controversies and Disputes for all the educational persons in a whole United State might be a bit too controversial and disputatious by nature.

What kind of reception might a disputatee receive if he called the Director of Disputes and asked for some direction? It might go like this:

Caller: Hello. Is this the Director of Disputes?

D of D: Who wants to know?

Caller: I have a dispute that might need some directing...

D of D: What makes you think so?

Caller: Well, I'm having this problem...

D of D: A problem isn't a controversy.

Caller: It can be.

D of D: Not necessarily.

Caller: But, I only...

D of D: Look, buster, are you trying to dispute me?

And it could go on like that. Instead of calling, an educational operative who needs to get a controversy or dispute directed should probably write to the Director. This being a government office, the applicant would undoubtedly be sent a form to fill out, asking him to check off whether the matter in question is a controversy or a dispute, location of the controversy or dispute by county, township, school district and census tract, date the controversy or dispute was initiated, Social Security numbers of the disputer and disputee or controversiator and controversiatee, and 68 pages of requests for other pertinent and impertinent data.

The form would help the Director decide whether to delegate the matter to the Deputy Director for Loud Arguing or the Deputy Director for Name Calling or the Deputy Director for Fist Fights or the Deputy Director for Hair Pulling, Kicking and Ancillary Disputatiousness.

Flash: Official Caught Not Stealing

The director of the public welfare program in Lindenwold, New Jersey, was forced to resign because she was caught unappropriating funds.

No, not misappropriating. She wasn't taking money out of the funds under her control. She was putting her own money in.

Her heart was in the right place, but some of the figures in her books weren't. Many of us who have tried to perform bookkeeping know how she felt. Rather than spend hours tracking down those few dollars missing among the debits and credits and decimal points, she found it easier to slip in a couple of bucks of her own and make the books balance.

When her effective and benevolent system was discovered, auditors, who are often inflexible in financial matters, told her never, ever, to donate money to public funds again and suggested that she resign.

It's just as well that she did. The woman obviously will never find a niche in politics or government.

First of all, she said she wanted the books to balance so that welfare recipients' checks would not be held up. Obviously, she has a soft heart. A political career requires a hard one at least, while cardiac absence is an even stronger qualification.

Second, she doesn't understand that in our political system, you cannot voluntarily give money to the government. The government has to take it by force.

In the good old days, princes and barons merely sent armed men around to collect from the citizens. Nowadays, our leaders use a more cruel form of coercion; they make us fill out incomprehensible forms, explained by interminable books of instructions.

Trying to donate money to the government can only confuse our elected officials in the same way that handing your wallet to a pickpocket would probably panic him.

There was a situation about 25 years ago in Philadelphia when a businessman offered to set up a souvenir stand at a tourist facility as a donation. He would install and staff the stand, donate the souvenirs to be sold, and turn 100 percent of the proceeds over to the city.

The city official responsible for the tourist site said he couldn't accept the offer without putting the job out for bids. Law required that such a franchise be awarded to the lowest bidder. When asked where he expected to find someone who would bid lower than zero, he got a glazed look in his eyes and whispered, "Just do it, and never tell anybody you talked to me."

The welfare director in Lindenwold faced the same attitude. Your typical public official becomes dazed and trembling when compelled to deal with honesty, unselfishness, and — good Lord! — a hand in the till doing input.

The auditors claim the woman may have injected as much as $5,000 of her own money into the welfare fund checking account.

She says she doesn't think it was nearly that much. But from what we know of her bookkeeping skills as compared to those of your average auditor, the five grand is most likely a close guess.

If she has any thoughts of re-entering the political world, there may still be hope for her. When asked if she would, knowing what she knows now, do the same thing again, she was quoted as replying: "I can't actually say yes or no. Probably."

Now, that's talking like a politician.

Diatribe Department

Every so often, even the calmest columnist feels compelled to issue a diatribe. The word means "a violent attack in words." A writer who tries to write humor usually diatribes with sarcasm and wise-guyism. The news items that inspired the outbursts in this chapter are now comatose, but the sentiments linger on.

The Bad Guys With the Guns

There was an outpouring of dismay and moral pondering in the news media when a guy from Baton Rouge (which is Louisianan for Red Stick) was acquitted of shooting a young fellow who came to his front door because the fellow was (1) a dang stranger, (2) one of them slanty-eyed furriners and (3) likely to do Gawd-knows what.

This Louisianan's stupid and cowardly action, and his acquittal of any wrongdoing, did not surprise most of us Yankees.

We understand that a guy from Baton Rouge (Red Stick) is more than likely a *Cou Rouge* (Red Neck) who is expected by custom to respond with severe hostility to the approach of anyone as exotically sinister as a *Japonais*, a *Negre*, or anybody else of a *couleur different*.

The Japanese, we are told by one news medium or another, do not understand that sturdy breed of American who is afraid of anyone different from himself, and often assuages that fear by employing a large pistol (or, in the old days, a rope with a noose at one end and a guy in a bedsheet at the other.)

Alternately, Americans don't understand a lot of peculiar behavior of the Japanese, like eating raw fish, committing hara kiri, making Godzilla movies or bombing Pearl Harbor.

One article about the Japanese reaction to the Baton Rouge atrocity was especially intriguing.

It was performed by a reporter for a Washington newspaper's Tokyo bureau.

The writer compared the case to the Rodney King beating in Los Angeles, but informed us that the Japanese did not riot in the streets after the Baton Rouge verdict.

"That's not how things are done in Japan," he advised us.

Really? What were all those news photos in recent decades showing Japanese riot police wearing helmets and body armor and carrying huge shields and batons (usually a *baton noir,* not *rouge*)? The depicted cops were often heaving tear gas at folks who were presumably doing something antisocial.

The article quoted a disappointed Japanese commentator as moaning, "Japan has always looked up to America. But now, which society is more mature?"

The writer then commented that this attitude reflects "the recent sharp decline in respect the Japanese have traditionally held toward the United States."

The words "always" and "traditionally" sound odd to Americans over 60 or so, who remember when the Japanese didn't look up to America.

Shortly before always, the Japanese looked down on America, particularly on the Sunday in 1941 when they looked down from airplanes and dropped bombs on Hawaii. Though traditionally polite, they discourteously neglected to mention in advance to the 2,300 Americans they killed that day that they had decided to declare war on us.

The Japanese may not often use guns to murder each other, but they've done a nice job of using them on other people. In a 40-year period that ended when we finally got their attention with a couple of A-bombs, the Japanese made war against Czarist Russia (and won), seized Korea, occupied Manchuria, invaded China and attacked the United States. It is widely believed that Japanese citizens shot one or two people during all that activity. None of the victims were at the front doors of the Japanese; they had to go looking for them.

Before they lose that traditional respect they always had for Americans, because of one trigger-happy xenophobe, the Japanese might try doing a body count of the foreigners they've shot dead.

Sports in the Land of the Free

The 76ers, a bunch of tall persons who play basketball for a living, decided a few weeks ago that they would like to have most of their games shown on cable television, instead of on airborne television as in the past.

This caused an immediate orgy of moaning and muttering. Editorials denounced the idea.

"The teams are forcing fans to decide whether to attend or watch games according to their wallets, not their loyalties," one editorialist bitterly editorialized.

Well, those of you born after 1940, get hold of your chairs, because the upcoming revelation may be a shock: Once upon a time, anyone who wanted to see a professional sporting event had to (gasp!) pay for it.

That's right, kiddies. Back in the dismal, misty days of yore, before there were fax machines, panty hose, Elvis impersonators, microwave ovens, rap music, Gatorade and other such amenities of civilization, there was no television.

People sat around in their spare time and read books, talked to each other, played with the kids and engaged in other primitive activities.

The old man could not sit down in the living room with a six-pack and an assortment of health-hazard snacks and watch a professional athletic competition by pushing a button.

If he wanted to see a performance by, let's say, the Philadelphia Eagles, a bunch of oversized persons who play a different game than the 76ers, he would have to dress up warmly and contrive some form of transportation to get himself to 21st and Lehigh or later to 34th and Spruce and enter an actual stadium, where the game would take place completely live and in person. And he would have to pay cash money for the privilege.

It never occurred to folks in those darkly ignorant times that some day the viewing of sports events free at home would be considered a God-given right like breathing, voting, getting a parking space in front of your house, getting tattooed, being eligible for the Publishers Clearing House sweepstakes, turning right on red, coffee breaks and other basic American freedoms.

But maybe that editorial was right. Maybe it's unfair for teams to force loyal fans to pay to watch them.

If fans of the 76ers have the right to see every slam-dunk transmitted directly into their living rooms, and not have to pony up cash, then the Phillies, the Eagles and the Flyers had better not deny anyone access to their games.

And what about the loyal fans of the Philadelphia Orchestra? Those musicians despicably expect people to pay to get into the Academy of Music. Why aren't they televising their symphonies so music lovers don't have to decide whether to listen to concerts according to their wallets?

Obviously, it isn't fair to make people pay to see rock concerts, rodeos, circuses, the animals at the Zoo, art museums, wrestling, ice shows or whatever. If the outcry about the 76ers is right, all public exhibitions should be on television.

And restaurants should give free meals to loyal fans who

want to eat them at home.

Why should we have to pay to be entertained? Isn't this a free country?

Let's Oppose Auto Control

While considering the viewpoint of the folks who oppose any kind of gun control, I suddenly realized that they should also fight against the registration of automobiles and the licensing of drivers.

The members of the NRA and other stalwart Americans claim that their position about guns comes from the Second Amendment to the Constitution.

NRA stands for National Rifle Association. It is actually an abbreviation of NRSPMGGLAODTCSHPA, which stands for the National Rifle, Shotgun, Pistol, Machine Gun, Grenade Launcher and Any Other Device That Can Shoot Holes in People Association.

And the Second Amendment, which praisers of the uncontrolled gun bind on their hands and write upon their doorposts, says: "A well-regulated militia being necessary to the security of a free State, the right of the people to keep and bear arms shall not be infringed."

The Constitution, of course, is intended to be interpreted and reinterpreted until it means what we want it to mean, as are the Ten Commandments, income tax codes, marriage vows, dieting instructions and election campaign promises.

So the Second Amendment undoubtedly means that automobiles should be as cheerfully uncontrolled as firearms.

In this era of high-speed mobility, a well-regulated militia would need transportation as well as guns. A liberal interpretation of that amendment, which is the only kind of Constitutional interpretation that's popular these days, would have to include motor vehicles along with firearms.

The government has been allowed to force manufacturers to put vehicle identification numbers on automobiles; states have made citizens register their cars and won't let anyone buy one without registration; and individual liberty has been compromised by placing age restrictions on vehicle use and compelling people to pass tests before getting a government license to drive.

Is this the way we do things in the Land of the Free?

Our youngsters are prevented from experiencing the character-building recreation of driving. The government keeps its bureaucratic eye on owners and users of vehicles. All this fascistic control of automobiles has not prevented highway deaths, has not stopped kids from driving illegally, and has not kept criminals from stealing and using automobiles.

Since the free and uncontrolled ownership of autos is outlawed, will it be long before only outlaws own autos?

The NRA, or other patriots, should speak out for the right of unregulated automobile ownership and the right of any American to drive, competent or not. A few people might get run over here and there, but our individual liberties would be preserved.

Or do I have this reversed? Should guns have manufacturers' numbers engraved on them, and government registration tags fastened to them, so stolen and misused ones can be identified? Should guns never be sold to children? Should gun users have to be tested by State Troopers to prove they can handle weapons safely before they are licensed to operate one?

And, Constitutionally speaking, should all gun-owners be required to join a well-regulated local militia unit of the National Guard, and attend frequently-scheduled drills?

Nah. That would be un-American.

The Kennedy Conspiracy

As a dedicated participant in the well-known media conspiracy to conceal the truth about the assassination of President Kennedy, I felt moved to produce these two reports when they were appropriate.

The Great Film Conspiracy

The movie called "JFK" was a big success. The film reveals that the assassination of President John F. Kennedy was actually the result of a vast conspiracy involving the Vice President, the FBI, the CIA, the Mafia, the Mills Brothers, the Junior Red Cross, Merv Griffin, the University of Michigan Marching Band, Warren Spahn, Mary Tyler Moore, several South Philly water ice vendors, Yo Yo Ma, the original cast of "Bye Bye Birdie" and Benji the Wonder Dog, to name just a few.

If films of that type are moneymakers, I have a few ideas for screenplays that should be worth big bucks.

The first is called "Custer." It documents that the death of Gen. George Custer was the result of a conspiracy. Does anyone really believe that those 3,000 Sioux acted alone?

President Grant and the Republicans were afraid that the Democrats would nominate the general for the presidency, so they conspired with the Pinkerton Detective Agency and the Bureau of Indian Affairs to get rid of him.

The barber's union wanted Custer out of the way because he was making long hair popular. Powerful business interests wanted to build a shopping mall on Indian land. An old woman in McComb City, Missouri, complained to friends that Custer had breathed near her after eating raw onions. Certain U. S. Army generals never liked Custer because he looked good in uniform.

So in June of 1876, Gen. Custer was sent into the Black Hills. The official account claims that he was killed because he had only 600 men and there were 3,000 Indians. But reliable witnesses, none of them questioned by the government and all of them dead now, saw another 12,874 Indians on a grassy knoll 87 miles down the Little Big Horn River.

And many experts, especially those who can convince a publisher to buy their books on the subject, discredit the theory advanced by a junior investigator for the Interior Department's Wildflower and Weed Division that a single arrow killed Custer, his orderly, his saddle-polisher and a dentist from Oregon who got lost on his way to the Centennial Exhibition.

Another screenplay is entitled "KK." It explodes the long-accepted theory that King Kong was killed by U. S. Army planes atop the Empire State Building solely because he was monkeying around on a large scale.

Kong had attracted the enmity of circus owners, who were afraid he would be too big a rival attraction. The owner of the Empire State Building was not happy that a big ape was climbing up the facade, and the window washers' union was incensed because Kong was getting toe marks on window-panes.

No rational person believes that King Kong could be destroyed by those rinkydink biplanes with war surplus machine guns. Witnesses were ignored when they reported puffs of smoke coming from the top of the Chrysler Building. Our film will clearly show that Kong was shot from there by a 75mm howitzer fired by a crew under the command of Fiorella LaGuardia.

Next, we start research on a screenplay about the Titanic. The single iceberg theory needs investigation.

Case Closed (If You Agree)

A lawyer named Gerald Posner has written a book called "Case Closed," which contends that Lee Harvey Oswald, all by himself, assassinated President John F. Kennedy.

This implies the improbability that the United States government has been caught telling the truth; that there are not dozens of people who have miraculously shared in keeping a secret for 30 years; that Arlen Specter (whose investigation explained some odd evidence in the shooting) has been discovered actually knowing what he's talking about; that Oliver Stone's film "J.F.K" was mostly "F.A.K.E"; that the FBI, the Mafia, the CIA, the Communists, the Pentagon, the Republicans, the Teamsters and Lyndon Johnson weren't closely allied after all, and other disturbing implications.

What is Posner trying to do? Take the bread out of the mouths of the children of that legion of writers who make a living grinding out books proving that Oswald wasn't the killer?

Or wasn't there. Or wasn't Oswald.

Or is he just trying to be controversial by maintaining that the Warren Commission may have known what it was doing?

Imagine giving any credence to a commission that included the Chief Justice of the United States, the two top government intelligence experts, a couple of Senators, a guy who would be president in a few years, and Cokie Roberts' father. Obviously a sneaky bunch.

Coincidental to Posner's book, about 800,000 pages of previously secret documents of the Warren Commission were made public. It was revealed that among the information craftily withheld from us was Marina Oswald's recipe for chicken soup and Lee Harvey Oswald's mother's accusation that the assassination was engineered by the Neiman-Marcus department store.

Posner's book also contradicts the contradicters who say that it is impossible to fire three shots with Oswald's rifle in the time taken by the assassination.

Would any of the critics volunteer to ride in a convertible down that Dallas street at the same speed as the presidential motorcade, while somebody in Oswald's window position tries to shoot them with the same type of rifle in the same amount of time? If they survived, it would prove they were right.

It's common for people to refuse to believe the official version of momentous events, and to denounce any evidence they don't like as part of the conspiracy and cover-up.

Look at the Lincoln assassination. It really was a conspiracy. Nine people besides John Wilkes Booth were implicated, and four of them were hanged.

But since then, hundreds of books and articles have claimed that Booth wasn't killed, but escaped, and have blamed the murder on the Secretary of War, the Democrats, the Republicans, the Confederate leaders, Vice President Andrew Johnson, and/or the Vatican.

Rejecting official positions and insisting that you know the real truth must make some folks feel pleasantly superior.

If you would like to share this heady feeling, pick an item to believe from the following:

Oswald was a patsy. The Holocaust never happened. Space aliens have crashed in the New Mexico desert. Bigfoot lives in the suburbs of Des Moines. Elvis isn't dead. Santa Claus is coming to town.

Lifestyles of the Ordinary

Those of us who rarely indulge in being rich and famous have our lifestyles picked at by strange outside forces. I dislike being organized, hypnotized, technologized or over-advised, and invite you to join me in such disliking by considering the following reports.

In Defense of Saving Junk

An advertisement came from a book club for a book entitled, "Not for Packrats Only," by somebody named Don Aslett who presumably is an expert on being orderly.

This book promises to tell how to "dejunk your life forever." It sounds more depressing than "Crime and Punishment," and I don't want to read it.

According to the description, this book threatens to compel you to "overcome your sentimental attachments to trash." The book lists "every possible excuse for not getting rid of all that junk ('It might come back in style' or 'But those were Aunt Annie's.')"

The book, sneers the advertising, will "enable you to live junk-free forever."

What a sad and dispiriting prospect. You might as well move to a Kurdish refugee camp.

People like this fellow Aslett arrogantly define junk in their own terms, and then scorn both it and those who appreciate it.

These haughty junk-definers consider as junk anything other people delight in keeping but they don't.

They snicker at people who collect baseball cards, gum wrappers, turpentine cans or nail parings, no matter how much pleasure the collectors derive from it.

They laugh out loud at people who keep scraps of wood, unmatched gloves, unidentified pieces of hardware, unused envelopes and other objects for which there is no immediate or pressing need. They can't grasp the obvious: that what they call junk is that invaluable kind of item that you save for 10 years and throw away two weeks before you need it.

But I will entertain small and simply-expressed bets that this guy Aslett has, somewhere in his dwelling place, a drawer or a box or something that contains miscellaneous items he would have a hard time assigning practical use or value. Anyone who doesn't keep irrational possession of at least one impractical item is either abysmally poor or an emotionless alien from the planet Vulcan.

And what better reasons to save things than the two mentioned above?

Things do come back in style. When the neckties get wide again, you get the tie box off the shelf, get out the ones you saved from the last time they were wide, and stick the narrow ones in to keep for a decade or two. And people who think that something new and expensive is more valuable than something that was Aunt Annie's have no soul.

Guys like Aslett will never feel the pleasure and satisfaction of knowing that stored safely in the basement are those odd nuts and bolts, half-empty paint cans, pieces of two-by-four and other materials from which you can make something, if you have to.

Also down there are that old Abbotts Dairy milk can, that croquet mallet, that wooden block and tackle, that jar of seashells, that Parcheesi game, that pair of shoe skates, that oil lamp, that box of Big Little Books from the Thirties — indeed, all kinds of delightful junk that just might come in handy. Or not. Who cares? It's there.

It may be possible to go too far. There are recluses who fill their houses with stacks of old Wall Street Journals and collections of baby grand pianos, goldfish skeletons and used birthday candles. But who are any of us, including Don Aslett, to deny them that pleasure and privilege?

There was one such recluse who never threw anything away, and had everything packaged and labeled. Among his effects, when he went to join the Big Collector in the Sky, was a box full of pieces of string.

The label on the box said, "String Too Short To Save." Think that over, Don Aslett.

You, Too, Can Be a Hypnotist

Several courses in hypnotism were advertised in our vicinity. One of them mentioned that the instructor is a member of the Hypnotists Guild, AFL-CIO.

Any management that has to deal with the hypnotists' union must have to be very careful. If hypnotists can't negotiate a tough contract, who can?

Management representatives who have to hammer out a contract with the hypnotists should observe the following rules:

1. Do not let the union leaders place on the table a small whirling wheel with a spiral pattern painted on it.

2. Leave the room if the hypnotists' business agent suggests that you are feeling drowsy.

3. Be suspicious of union people who uses the phrases, "Concentrate. Your eyelids are getting heavy. You are in my power."

Those of us who are not hypnotists may have an exaggerated view of what they can do, or make other people do. But it's hard to avoid worrying about it.

Once I was invited to a hypnotists' banquet. (Newspaper writers get invited to a lot of peculiar events. I was also invited to a nudists' picnic once. I told them that if I didn't have anything on that afternoon, I might come.) I didn't go to the hypnotists' banquet, either. But it must be a great job to be chairman of a hypnotists' banquet. Think of the profit you could make. You charge 75 bucks a ticket. You get the guests all seated, and serve them each a couple of Ritz crackers and a glass of water. But first you put the whole group into a trance, and tell them, "You are having filet mignon, asparagus hollandaise, potatoes au gratin and champagne. When I snap my fingers, you will awake refreshed and remember nothing."

Another of the recent advertisements for a hypnotism course began, "Become a Clinical Hypnotherapist in just one weekend!"

The whole course was scheduled from a Friday evening through Sunday in a hotel in South Philadelphia. The total time was 18 hours.

"Graduates of this 3-Day Seminar will receive a Certified Hypnotherapist diploma, and will be eligible for registration with and certification by the American Board of Hypnotherapy," the advertising brochure said.

The last half hour of the schedule was devoted to "Strategies for Starting a Hypnotherapy Business."

"Begin your practice as soon as you graduate," the brochure suggested.

I hope the graduates frame the diploma and hang it in a prominent place visible to new customers. If I ever feel the need to be hypnotized, I'd want to know that the person about to mess with my mind had been trained for 18 hours, and I'd leave to go looking for somebody more qualified, who had studied the subject for maybe a week or two.

The instructor's listed credentials included the fact that he is certified as a Firewalk Instructor by the Firewalking Institute of Research and Education. Do the firewalkers have a union, too? They could really take management over the coals.

We're Getting Obsoleted Again

They're doing it to us again. The technical people who figure out how to record music are threatening to make our record-playing equipment obsolete.

They're bragging about new ways to record music. They're hustling the Digital Audio Tape (DAT), the Minidisc (MD) and the Digital Compact Cassette (DCC), any and each of which are hoorahed to have advantages over the Compact Disc (CD). All this makes me Positively Outraged (PO'd).

How many times are the developers of recording systems going to force us to go out and buy new machinery? How many boxes of old-fashioned records are we going to store in the attic or try to unload at a yard sale?

When we were young, music was neatly provided to us on 78 rpm records, the way God intended. We didn't even know how many revolutions they revoluted per minute. We just cranked up the Victrola, carefully lowered the needle arm onto the first groove, and leaned back and listened to music. Or rolled back the parlor carpet and danced.

Some technical changes started to creep up on us, but they were real improvements. The crank was replaced by electricity. Automatic changers came along so we could lean back and listen longer, or dance longer, without messing with the machine.

But just when we got good at the leaning back and the dancing, the record industry introduced the 45 rpm record.

The industry carefully explained the advantages of the new speed record with a smaller diameter and a bigger hole. The music was going to sound better. Nobody explained that there was also an advantage to the industry, although record owners figured that out all by themselves: everybody had to go out and spend money on new equipment.

Then came the bigger than 78, slower than 45 leap in technology, the 33 rpm record. The sound was better, the music played longer, the old equipment was obsolete, the new investment was expensive, the manufacturers were counting their money. Once more, music lovers were stuck.

Then came cassette tape. They got us again.

Let's not even think about eight-track tapes. That phenomenon slid through the obsolescence chain so quickly that some people didn't have time to provide the manufacturers with their profits on that new invention. They flopped right into the current phase — the CD.

Anybody over 60 who wants to listen to music in the living room armchair has seen the recording method change five times so far, and has had to buy new equipment three or four times at least.

Not only do the recording people maliciously keep inventing wonderful new stuff we absolutely can't do without, they insist on phasing out the old. For a while it was possible to buy phonograph equipment that would play three speeds of records, but now nobody wants to sell us a new turntable that still knows how to roll around at our beloved old 78 speed.

Nor has anyone sold those 45 rpm phonographs with the big fat spindle for a long while. New turntables, if they are willing to turn at that speed at all, are equipped with a little round plastic adapter that has been carefully designed to fall down behind the furniture and disappear.

How long will it be before Baby Boomers with giant collections of 33 and 45 rpm records will find that, when their old record player breaks down, no new equipment is available to play their Elvis or Beatles originals? Then they'll know how old timers feel about their Glen Miller or Ted Weems 78s.

CDs have taken over now. Tapes are running second and falling back. And now come the DATs, MDs and DCCs, which will need another new, expensive kind of equipment to play them.

Will CDs be obsolete in another decade? How many useless music machines must a person trash in one lifetime?

But let's not talk about it too loudly. We might give other industries ideas. Suppose light bulb technology changed every 10 years or so, and we had to replace all our lamps. Suppose they widened all the bread and we all had to buy new toasters.

Getting Ready for Winter

Winter will soon arrive, an annual event. Actually, it might be slightly alarming if it didn't happen some year.

It is now time to winterize your house. Therefore it is time for news media busybodies to give you advice on the subject, because it is always hard for members of the press to think of something to write about or members of the transmitter something to talk about, and we can fall back on winterizing once a year or so.

So let us now summarize how to winterize, thus beginning the season with a bad pun.

One of the first tasks for a homeowner as winter approaches is taking care of the storm windows. There are three types of storm windows:

Type 1. The old wooden ones that hang from funny looking square hooks, that you take down in the spring and scribble their location in pencil on the edges before you put them in the garage, so you will know which window they go on when it's time to put them back.

Then, as you diligently begin to winterize stuff, you drag out the windows and read the edges and see things written there like "L-BR-2" and can't remember whether that means the top of the left bedroom window or the bottom of the lower back room window.

Experienced homeowners know that it doesn't matter what the scribble is trying to convey. Storm windows never fit where you think they should go anyhow.

Type 2. The modern built-in aluminum kind, that slide up and down along with screens in efficiently designed tracks, except that they are stuck and cannot be moved unless you can grasp and pull back on little bitty clips that were designed to be held by fingers the size of an eight-month-old baby's but with the strength of crocodile jaws.

Type 3. The storm windows you never got around to taking down at all last spring, so they are still in place and don't have to be messed with. This is highly recommended.

Another good move, winterizing-wise, is to bring in the garden hose that has been fastened all summer to the outdoor faucet. Your typical hose connection will have bonded to the faucet with the grip of Arnold Schwarzenegger, but can be unscrewed by the average homeowner with applications of muscle, patience and appropriate muttering of rude language.

As the heating season approaches, it is also customary to start worrying about fuel bills. The cost of fuel is determined by a committee of Arabs, Texans and other rich foreigners after assessing the factors that make oil and gas prices go up. (There are no factors that make fuel prices go down.)

Fuel prices go up if any of the following conditions occur: The weather is unusually cold. The weather is unusually warm. There is a shortage of oil and gas. There is an oversupply of oil and gas.

The rising cost of home heating can be beaten by carefully following these simple steps: 1. Insulate your house. 2. Set your thermostat at 68 degrees. 3. Sell your house and move to Tampa.

The Thing of Shapes to Come

When the warm weather of early summer arrives, people are required by ancient custom to appear in public, at pools and beaches, in bathing suits.

Virtually no adult American person thinks he or she looks good in a bathing suit.

The number of persons who think they look good in bathing suits is smaller than the number who intend to vote Republican in November solely because they are desperately eager to retain Dan Quayle. (Yes. There is a number that small. It is obscure and known only to a few mathematicians.)

Those who think they look good in bathing suits include fashion models, body builders of all sexes, wishful-thinking teenagers, people who equate maximum exposure of anatomy with attractiveness and other deluded narcissists.

The rest of us are divided into three classes of bathing suit wearers: Those who don't much care how they look, those who will go to great lengths to avoid being seen in a bathing suit, and those who have resolved to do something about their physiques.

Both men and women fall into these groups. The men generally either have the problem of the area just above the top of the trunks appearing like the prow of your standard promotional blimp, and/or having legs that have both the contours and color of PVC gas pipe.

The women have many more problems, since much is expected of them. The average American woman has been brainwashed into thinking she should look perfect in a bathing suit. The brainwashing is performed mostly by men and fashion magazines. The men are fairly consistent in admiring women with a maximum of figure and a minimum of bikini. But the magazines biannually change the rules of perfection.

The ideal form promulgated by the magazines is the form of fashion models. Usually these are women carefully selected because they have shapes that make them suitable for use as bookmarks.

In occasional decades, the genetic engineers who create these unnaturally shaped women, snickering behind their hands, suddenly dictate that women should have hips, or bosoms, or both. This is a joke on all the ordinary, non-model, women who have painfully adjusted their diet, exercise and elastic garments to conform to the previous officially-accepted shape.

There are among us rare human beings: women who don't care that they don't look like the cover of Vogue, or men who are content to bulge where Arnold Schwarzenegger contracts and be thin where he bulges. This is due either to placid self-confidence or depressed despair.

The avoiders can be found on the beach in large shapeless garments, or insisting that they have to stay home and weed the impatiens bed while the neighbors are off for the swim club, or using similar subterfuges.

Those who want to do something about it are found purchasing multiple fitness club memberships, going on desperate diets consisting of combinations recommended by sympathetic relatives (nothing but sweet gherkins and pineapple juice for breakfast and lunch for two weeks, plus sensible dinners with no meat or starches and at least one Vandalia onion.)

It's no use. While the women try to conform, the fashion designers are already working on next year's new shape. And the men, when not exercising, are ingesting summer food and drink that will expand next year's abdomen.

Temporarily, Some Sanity

Pleading insanity is very popular among those of us who are now and again charged with murder. (You know who you are.)

Folks who like to pass the time by torturing casual acquaintances down in the basement or converting visitors to their premises into cold cuts will sit serenely in a courtroom while their lawyers announce that they are not really all that guilty because they are insane, or at least were in that lamentable condition when they happened to indulge in unacceptable behavior. The rest of the populace seems to be ambivalent about these protestations of conveniently momentary mental illness.

When a Jeffrey Dahmer or Hannibal Lecter or Charles Manson or Gary Heidnik engages in some ghastly activity, discussions held in barrooms, kitchens, office lunchrooms, senior citizen centers, back yards, Sunday School classes and other repositories of wisdom always reach the consensus that the guy is thoroughly off his nut.

But when the perpetrator goes into a courtroom and says that he, too, believes he is crazy, the members of the aforementioned discussion groups denounce the suggestion. How dare this uncontrolled loony try to evade his justly-deserved megayears in the slammer by claiming to be an uncontrolled loony?

Yammer as we might, the idea of temporary insanity is here to stay.

If an accusee can convince a jury that he or she experienced a brief, shining moment of medically-authenticated insanity while stuffing Aunt Louella into a dumpster, that means being sentenced to loll about in a hospital with hopes of being pronounced well again and sent home some sunny day. This is highly preferable to a lifetime of license plate manufacture.

With the right lawyers and doctors earning their keep in the defendant's corner, it seems to work out favorably very often for homicidal but part-time maniacs.

Isn't it a shame, though, that temporary insanity cannot be pleaded in some of the more normal pursuits of daily existence?

"I'm sorry I don't have my homework, Miss Hinkelplucker, but I suffered an attack of temporary insanity just as I left school yesterday, and I didn't recover until I got back in the classroom this morning."

"Sorry I was late for work, Mr. Rumpbooter, but the frightening jangle of the alarm clock shocked me into a state of insanity, and I rolled over and went back to sleep."

"I know I told you I loved you last evening, Mary-Gertrude, but I suffer from these temporary mental lapses when I can't be held accountable for my actions."

"Well, you see, officer, yellow lights cause me episodes of temporary insanity that usually end just after I pass the red light."

So far, it seems that only murderers can get away with this kind of excuse.

And if it could be applied to other misdemeanors and peccadillos, a temporary insanity plea would still be of no help to the unfortunate rest of us who are stable; that is, we are either sane all the time or crazy all the time.

I believe that what I have just written makes sense. If not, it was not my fault. It was produced during a few minutes of temporary sanity.

The Newest in Old Clothes

An advertisement for knit summer shirts promises that they don't need to be "broken in", because they are "weathered mesh". The ad explains that no two of these new shirts are exactly alike, and that there is "frosting" around the plackets that is unique to each shirt, because they have been washed "for just the right duration".

In other words, the new shirts are old shirts before you buy them. Apparently, the current generation of clothing wearers considers garments that are beat up upon purchase to be more valuable than those in good condition.

It started a while back with those pre-faded jeans. Lately, not only fading has become fashionable, but also holes in the knees and in other more embarrassing places. Jeans that are faded, frayed and punctured sell for high prices, to people whose daddies used to hope their jeans wouldn't get in that condition and have to be thrown away.

Now a fashion-plate can buy a brand new beat-up shirt to go with those brand new beat-up jeans.

Will this trend pass along to other products? Will pre-dented new automobiles be offered in the showrooms? Will a Chevy with a tinge of rust around the door edges and fenders be considered more stylish than a shiny new one?

Maybe the marketing experts are at this very moment planning to introduce already run-down batteries, pre-sipped root beer, holey socks, previously sneezed-in tissues, slightly wilted floral arrangements, charred firewood, partially melted ice cubes, semi-deflated helium balloons, short-life light bulbs, dull knives and somewhat defrosted ice cream.

The prospects seem endless to develop products that appeal to people who want to buy their clothing already in tatters.

Not only is it considered elegant to wear clothing that would create bad will if you tried to give it to Goodwill. Today, youthful fashion requires that clothing be too big and too loud.   When it comes to loudness, men's summer clothes these days feature fearsome colors and belligerent patterns. The racks in the men's area of department stores look like thrift shops for unemployed clowns.

And as for bigness, stuff that isn't pre-faded or pre-ripped, to be up-to-date, is required to be baggy, droopy and dangly.

Recently I saw a shirt that said on the label that the size was "small." The label also reported that the garment was "oversized." So if the style is to wear an oversized shirt, why make small sizes at all? Why not just sell small people medium shirts?

Obviously I don't understand, sitting here in my old fashioned unfaded clothing that fits, with no holes in it that I know of.

Some Arguable Differences

A researcher at the University of Denver, financed by a government grant, says he has discovered a major difference between men and women. (Stop snickering; take this seriously.)

He has discovered that men and women argue differently.

His research team followed 150 couples from courtship through the first 10 years of marriage.

How this nosiness was accomplished, I don't know, since I have not read the whole study, only a short report about it in Modern Maturity magazine. But a lot of Oldfashioned Immaturity seems to have been uncovered.

The report doesn't say what differences these academic busybodies detected by spying on couples while they were in the accepted matrimonial process of disagreeing. What the 10-year study probably found is that men are always right, while on the other hand, women are always right.

The article says that "couples who learned to argue fairly and effectively" decreased their chances of divorce by 50 percent.

There's fresh insight in that. Proficient arguers always knew that fairness was a basic requirement. No argument is complete without at least one party bellowing, "That's not fair!" about something the opponent said.

But here's a new rule an arguer can be caught breaking. Extra points go to the first combatant who hollers, "You're not arguing effectively, you skunk!"

Instead of outlining the sexual variations in arguing, which might be interesting, the article merely tries to tell us what to do about them.

"Set aside a specific time when interruptions are minimal to talk about problems", it suggests. All right, you argumentative couples out there. Schedule a regular time slot for arguing.

"How about every Thursday at 11 P. M.?"

"You know I always watch the news on television at 11 o'clock."

"You just like to drool over that blonde anchorwoman on channel 10."

"Well, at least she doesn't have her hair up in curlers and white stuff all over her face at 11 o'clock."

"Well, the anchorman isn't holding a Bud in one hand and scratching himself with the other like some people I know, either."

Okay, let's move on to some other suggestions in the article: "When one person is talking, the other listens," it recommends.

What? What kind of an argument would that be? Both people talking at once is a basic procedure among competent arguers.

"The listener should then paraphrase the speaker's remarks to make sure he/she understands", the article goes on.

"Now, let me paraphrase your asinine remark to make sure I understand your stupid viewpoint. You say my mother gives you a pain in the butt. Let me point out, fairly and effectively, that if you got off the aforementioned butt and were nice to her once in a while..."

"Summing up what you just said, do you imply that I am not nice to the old bat? She hasn't said a civil word to me in 10 years. You can ask those guys from the University of Denver who are filming this through the mail slot."

"Go ahead. Keep it up. You're arguing fairly and effectively on purpose to reduce our chances of divorce 50 percent, you dirty so-and-so".

It's Music Time; Plug Your Ears

A heavy metal rock band took the sensible step of passing out earplugs to the audience at one of its concerts.

The band, which uses the cheerful name Megadeth, distributed 13,000 pairs of earplugs to its assembled admirers in a San Francisco auditorium. The generosity was attributed to the band's wish to support an organization called HEAR, which is devoted to the probably lost cause of preventing hearing loss among rock music fans.

The earplug plan is a step in the right direction. But wouldn't it be simpler if the band just played a little less loud?

Alternately, the 13,000 people at that San Francisco concert could have stayed home. This would have saved their ears and also their cost of a ticket, and would have saved Megadeth the price of all those earplugs.

And after that phase of the ear-saving campaign, the next step for heavy metal bands, and other allegedly musical groups whose decibel level approximates peak production time in a steel mill, could be to stop performing altogether and go out and get honest work.

Or perhaps the world of the arts is reaching a new, esoteric plateau here. We may be seeing the beginning of a trend.

First, people will go to a concert and wear earplugs, and not hear any of the noise that the performers stubbornly insist is music. Next, blindfolds will be handed out at art exhibits so nobody has to look at what passes for paintings and sculpture these days.

At plays, operas, ballets and movies, the audiences will have both their ears and their eyes covered in order to appreciate the full absence of sensation. At the movies, some duct tape over the mouths may be required to keep the crowd from enjoying popcorn.

Entertainment-lovers will be able to savor this new technique at home by wearing earplugs while playing the stereo full blast. (If it's not stereo, will they need only one earplug?)

Finally, they can add a blindfold, turn on the television and savor a complete multi-sense non-experience.

Megadeth may go down in history as the group that launched this bright new approach to entertainment.

Please excuse me if I sound doubtful about all this, but I find it hard to warm up to an outfit called Megadeth in the first place. Names like Megadeth and the Grateful Dead and Nine Inch Nails and Led Zeppelin automatically make me begin thinking earplug.

That's probably true of any of us who grew up listening to music of organizations with names like Shep Fields and his Rippling Rhythm, or Alvino Rey and his Singing Guitar, or the Sentimental Gentlemen of Swing. Even when rock and roll first intruded on our eardrums, the small clots of mediocre musicians tended to call themselves things like Danny and the Juniors, Dion and the Belmonts, Dicky Doo and the Don'ts and other non-threatening names.

That musical era, which may have been Light Plastic, has been replaced by Heavy Metal, and we have reached the level where popular music can't be enjoyed without stopping up our ears. It's an outcome a lot of us have been predicting for years.

Distant People

It is interesting to examine other cultures. Whether other cultures feel the same about us, I don't know.

Having an Enemy for Dinner

A report from a small West African country mentioned that government security forces were believed to have eaten a political opponent they arrested.

I am not revealing the name of the country in question, because it is probable that most of its inhabitants rarely devour anybody, even political opponents.

And in fairness, the security agents are not accused of consuming the entire politician, but only a few of his more important internal organs (although the effect on the politician was probably not much different than if he had been table d'hoted instead of merely ala carted.)

So I am withholding the identity of the country, because I would not want to offend or hold up to ridicule any of its more genteel citizens who might be living in the United States and are neither eaters nor eatees in this or similar situations.

Nor would I want to annoy any of that government's agents who are among us and might be inclined to retaliate for my pointing out the unpleasant event, and might be waiting in the shrubs for me after work some night armed with A-1 Sauce, a charcoal grille and various sharp-edged kitchen implements.

And I don't want to encourage stereotypes. Europeans and

Americans often have peculiar ideas about the behavior of residents of emerging nations on unfamiliar continents.

An old-time foreign correspondent once told me about attending a press conference back in the 1950s for the sophisticated, Oxford-University-educated premier of a newly independent African nation (not the one in question here.) An insensitive reporter from a European newspaper stupidly asked the premier if there were still cannibals in his country.

"No," the premier answered wryly. "We ate the last one months ago."

The report of the gustatorial disposal of a political opponent in that other, less enlightened land gives a certain odd reassurance to Americans at election time, when politics are frequently perpetrated at polling places here and there.

Americans are inclined to worry a lot about the nastiness of election campaigns. We complain about negative television advertising, dislike name calling and dirty tricks, and sadly use the term mud-slinging.

But even at their worst moments, our politicians have not yet resorted to fricasseeing opponents. Republicans may never invite Democrats to share lunch, or vice versa, but neither do they propose that their opponents become lunch.

Political scientists are divided on the question of whether Democrats or Republicans are lower in the food chain. Both major parties find the smaller parties unpalatable, but strictly in ideals and not on a comestible level.

Even J. Edgar Hoover never suggested eating communists.

Perhaps we should feel grateful that we live in a land in which, when a politician complains that his opponent disagrees with him, Pepto Bismol won't solve the problem.

Help for the Undiscovered

A previously undiscovered tribe has been discovered in New Guinea. A regional police patrol came upon this group of folks loitering in some remote mountains.

That kind of announcement comes out of New Guinea every so often. There seem to be a lot of wrong-thinking tribes wandering around in the boonies there, obstinately remaining undiscovered and acting like they enjoy their undiscoveredness.

Civilized people naturally resent that attitude, and work furiously to put a stop to it.

The government instantly rushed in supplies the 79 members of the tribe are badly lacking. Clothes, for one thing; these undiscovered ladies and gents were going about naked, deliberately defying all sorts of laws and customs they had never heard of.

The benevolent government also sent them cooking utensils and tools.

Most important of all, missionaries from the nearest settlement were on their way immediately to build a church for the tribespeople.

If past experience tells us anything (and it does, of course, but we rarely listen) the missionaries will also be insisting that the tribe members put on the provided clothing and in general begin behaving like somebody who has been discovered.

Missionaries have traditionally exceeded their original commission. Jesus instructed His followers to go out into all the world and preach the gospel. But a superficial search of the New Testament doesn't turn up any report that He also told them to make everybody wear trousers.

We have to hope that the government agents and the missionaries will get together to explain the cooking utensils and tools to the lucky recipients.

The tribespersons might get the utensils and the clothes confused. A sauce pan can make a dandy hat.

The government down in Papua New Guinea has had a lot of experience with handling undiscovered tribes and getting them suitably un-undiscovered. We can be confident that the 79 new discoverees will soon enter the mainstream of the 20th century, appropriately using microwave ovens, cordless screwdrivers, roll-on deodorant and Nike running shoes.

Like most of these unknown tribes who suddenly turn up in the bushes, this is a small group. With only 79 members, they have barely enough members to put together a decent bowling league.

It's not hard to ship in enough clothes and utensils and tools to satisfy the requirements of 79 people who have just been informed that they have been discovered.

What would the government there ever do if some explorer suddenly bumped into a tribe with 347,823 members? There would probably have to be a tax increase to finance all the axes, stew pots and underdrawers that custom dictates must be presented to an unknown tribe.

A final thought: at this moment, the 79 members of that tribe may be formulating plans to teach the other six billion people on the planet how to get along nicely without clothes, cooking utensils, tools or a church. They may think they have discovered us.

Our Last War
(At This Writing)

In August of 1990, the Hon. Saddam Hussein, president of Iraq, caused considerable annoyance by sending some representatives of his army next door to Kuwait to see how much stuff they could carry away. Iraq at the time had the third largest army in the world, although the country's population was not much larger than New York State's. You can see why Saddam wanted to keep the army busy.

As Saddam's army took from Kuwait just about everything except what Iraq needs the most, a U to put decently after that naked Q on its end, the following information was dispersed.

Meet Saddam's Role Model

Some journalists who write about Saddam Hussein (and just about all of them do these days except cooking columnists and ballet critics) say that he is an admirer of King Nebu chadnezzar.

In case you don't recognize the name, Saddam Hussein is the boss of Iraq, which is a foreign country, and seems to be getting more foreign all the time, the way Saddam runs it.

In case you don't recognize the other name, Nebuchadnezzar was the king of Babylon from 605 to 562 B.C. We are talking here about Nebuchadnezzar II, and not Nebuchadnezzar I, who ruled from 1124 to 1103 B.C. and was the one who smote the Elamites.

Nebuchadnezzar II did some occasional smiting, too, but he was better known as the guy who hung the Hanging Gardens of Babylon, which were declared one of the Seven Wonders of the World by whoever it is who announces what the most wonderful wonders are.

Babylon was an ancient city about 60 miles south of Baghdad, where Saddam Hussein currently sits around thinking up lies to tell the United Nations. Writers say that he talks about rebuilding the Hanging Gardens of Babylon as a tourist attraction. Nebuchadnezzar seems to be his role model.

So, if we want to understand Saddam Hussein, a dubious thing to want, we should examine the life of Nebuchadnezzar. Let us now either do that or go bowling, whichever you prefer.

Nebuchadnezzar, as you probably recall, was the son of Nabopolassar, who helped the Medes smite the Assyrians. Smiting came naturally to folks in those days. Unfortunately, the smitees often did not remain smitten, so there was carrying on and confusion all the time.

Nebuchadnezzar conquered Judah in 586 B.C., which got him mentioned in eight different books of the Old Testament and one in the Apocrypha. (Some people will do anything for publicity.)

He captured Jerusalem and put King Zedekiah's eyes out. His army burned the Temple and all the big buildings, and carried back to Babylon, according to the Old Testament, "the pots, and the shovels, and the snuffers, and the spoons, and all the vessels of brass" not to mention 5,400 vessels of gold and silver. This will not surprise the Kuwaitis, who are probably still waiting to get their snuffers back.

One night, Nebuchadnezzar had a dream, and wanted his advisers to explain what it meant. They asked him what he dreamed. He said he couldn't remember, but they should interpret the dream anyway, or else "ye shall be cut in pieces, and your houses shall be made a dunghill." It's easy to understand what Saddam sees in him.

He could be a nice guy at times. After Daniel, one of the Jewish kids he had captured and dragged to Babylon, interpreted his dream, he ordered his servants to "offer an oblation and sweet odours unto him." When was the last time anybody saw Saddam Hussein handing out sweet odours?

Not long after, Nebuchadnezzar tossed three of Daniel's buddies into a "burning fiery furnace" and turned up the gas so it was "one seven times more than it was wont to be heated." The trio escaped, but the whole episode doesn't speak well of Nebuchadnezzar.

At the end, Nebuchadnezzar went a little bit nutty, "and did eat grass as oxen," so if Saddam Hussein patterns himself after old Nebby, maybe he should just be put out to pasture.

The Return Of Babylon

At the beginning of 1991, the United States decided to send General Norman Schwartzkopf to Kuwait. He single-handedly defeated several billion Iraqi soldiers, liberated Kuwait and got interviewed by Barbara Walters, all simultaneously. However, Saddam Hussein took the attitude that just because he was beaten, that didn't mean he had lost. Thus, he cleverly kept his name in the news long enough for the following further revelations to be revealed.

Saddam Hussein Al-Takriti, who is president of Iraq by trade, has been getting a lot of attention again.

Saddam's admiration for the late King Nebuchadnezzar II was discussed in this column last year, when we were last being annoyed by assorted Saddamian activities. Let's not again go into the details of the antisocial behavior of Nebuchadnezzar between 605 and 562 B. C. You could look it up.

But last year's essay touched only slightly on the fact that

Saddam Hussein aspires to rebuild the ancient city of Babylon, which was Nebuchadnezzar's home town.

Babylon under Nebuchadnezzar controlled what is now Iraq, Kuwait, Israel, Syria, Jordan and Lebanon. Nebuchadnezzar captured Jerusalem and enslaved the Jews. What an inspiration he must be to Saddam Hussein. In 539 B. C., King Cyrus of Persia conquered Babylon, and the place was never the same.

When Saddam Hussein became president of Iraq in 1979 and thoughtfully made further elections unnecessary by executing his 22 most likely rivals, he decided to rebuild Babylon, the remnants of which are about 60 miles from his hangout in Baghdad, as the carpet flies.

At the same time, Saddam also decided that Iraq should start arguing with Iran next door, and in less than a year they were enjoying a full course war with all the trimmings. In 1982, while the Iraqis and Iranians were busy duking it out, Saddam's government published a booklet about ancient Babylon that said on the back cover, "Archeological Survival of Babylon is a Patriotic, National and International Duty."

By 1986, the modern governor of Babylon was telling reporters, "The president has signed a blank check to reconstruct the ancient city and revive the marvelous shape it had before the Persian aggression which destroyed it more than 20 centuries ago."

Persia, you see, is now Iran. Some folks can hold a grudge for 2,500 years.

Ignoring the protests of his archaeologists, Saddam Hussein rebuilt Babylonian structures right on top of the remains of the real ones. He recreated part of Nebuchadnezzar's palace and throne room, an ancient street, a 4,000 seat amphitheater, some assorted temples, and a reduced-scale version of the fancy Ishtar Gate. (Ishtar was goddess of love in most of the Middle East in those days, but doubled as goddess of both love and war in Babylon, which must have kept her pretty busy.)

Among the restored ruins are snack bars, rest areas and a guest house to entertain foreign visitors.

For the reconstruction, bricks were made to match the ancient ones. The original bricks had Nebuchadnezzar's name imbedded in them; the new ones have the name of guess who?

Saddam wants to redevelop the fabled Hanging Gardens, and offered a million dollar prize to any Iraqi who figures out how they were irrigated in ancient times. The Tower of Babel was reputed to be on the same site as Babylon, and Saddam has considered reconstructing that, too, although the blueprints don't seem to be on file anywhere.

In 1987 and 1988, Saddam staged big Babylonian Festivals, attended by visitors from all over the world, with entertainment by musicians, opera singers and ballet dancers from nine European countries.

The Iraqis invited Madonna from the United States to perform, but she declined. Just as well, too. Many men over there don't like women to have their faces uncovered in public, and Madonna's face is often uncovered from the toes up.

The World of Science

Science doesn't really have its own world. But then, who does?

How Scientific Literacy Evolved

Timothy Ferris is a science writer, and one of the best. He started out as a journalist, but there is evidence that he has started thinking like a scientist, which is too bad.

Back in the days when he was teaching journalism at Brooklyn College, a book he wrote included an anecdote that intrigued me, about a Russian mathematician who figured out the distance from Earth (or at least from Russia) to Heaven.

In 1905, during the Russian-Japanese war, the Russian churches organized some heavy duty praying, asking God to visit His (or Her) wrath upon Japan. And 18 years later, Japan was devastated by an earthquake.

The mathematician, being familiar with Einstein but not science fiction, believed that nothing can go faster than the speed of light. Prayer, he reasoned, being powerful stuff, probably goes as fast as anything. Since the round trip took 18 years, it obviously was nine years at light-speed for the prayers to reach the Almighty and another nine for the requested wrath to be delivered.

That means that Heaven is nine light years away, which is 52.902 trillion miles, give or take a couple of feet.

Meanwhile, Timothy Ferris, who is now teaching astronomy at Berkeley, disappointed me in the introduction to a book he edited called "The World Treasury of Physics, Astronomy and Mathematics."

"That scientific illiteracy exists is not in doubt," he wrote. "A survey conducted for the National Science Foundation in the mid 1980s found that only one-third of the American public understands what a molecule is, that nearly half reject the theory of evolution, and that only one in 10 can distinguish astronomy from astrology."

He is comparing an apple, an orange and an apple. Lacking knowledge about molecules or astronomers is not comparable to rejecting a theory.

Ferris is taking the attitude, which trickles through the scientific community, that disagreement with current thinking is ignorance.

Ever since human intelligence evolved, or was created, the conventional thinkers have eagerly adopted the current theory and laughed at anyone who insisted that the previous idea was the correct one, or at anyone who had a new idea not yet widely accepted.

If you want to be considered scientifically literate, always agree with the experts.

In 1859, the year Charles Darwin published "The Origin of Species," it would have been all right for the scientifically literate to snicker at his ideas about evolution. They were new ideas, and equally snickerable with the old theory of Erasmus Darwin, Charlie's grandfather, that acquired characteristics can be inherited. The scientifically literate knew then, and still know, that grandpop was wrong.

It was also in the scientifically enlightened year 1859 that Dr. John Lightfoot of Cambridge University corrected the pronouncement made by Archbishop James Ussher in 1654 that the world was created on Oct. 22 in 4004 B.C.

It was actually Oct. 23, he revealed.

Did Dr. Lightfoot know what a molecule is?

How to Make Science Simple

There are a lot of things in our culture these days that are complicated and hard to understand, like astronomy and physics and income tax forms and Tom Clancy novels and Eastern European politics, so it's always nice to come across a succinct and clear explanation of something or other.

Such a rare moment of revelation came in an article by a Washington newspaper writer about the discovery of a whole bunch of gamma rays popping up somewhere in space, which astrophysicists are unable to explain.

(Don't worry. Those rays will be explained soon. Astrophysicists can come up with a theory to explain anything. And if they can't explain it, they just say it isn't important.)   The writer from Washington said that the astrophysicists usually blame neutron stars for dumping messes of extra gamma rays into our galaxy. Then came the wonderful explanation. This is really what she wrote (I can show you the clipping):

"Neutron stars are ordinary stars that have collapsed, compressing matter with the mass of the sun into an object about the size of a metropolitan area, giving off gargantuan amounts of energy."

That's terrific. It all becomes clear now.

For years, I've been wandering around, trying my best to picture a neutron star, a big mass in a small object. I tried imagining a 300 pound football player compressed into a jockey, a bowling ball sized down to be fired from an air rifle, the national debt reduced to a size I could pay off. None of it worked. I just couldn't envision a neutron star.

It was starting to bother me.

Then, along came the analogy that did the trick. All you have to do is imagine the sun compressed to the size of a metropolitan area.

This obviously should be done in stages. Start out by picturing the sun as the size of the New York metropolitan area. That's an easy first step. The sun is one of the few things bigger than the New York metropolitan area, if you include Newark and Elizabeth. I'm not sure why anybody would want to include Newark and Elizabeth, but New York's metropolitan area tends to do that. You never know what New Yorkers are likely to do.

After you have mentally compressed the sun to the size of New York, you can start scaling it down. Try the Philadelphia metropolitan area next (don't forget to include Wilmington and Trenton, the way the federal government does when it decides where not to send money for mass transit).

Now you're on a roll. Mentally squash the sun to the size of Cleveland. Got it? Now, Columbus, Ohio. Now, Austin, Texas. Wichita. Des Moines. Spokane. Peoria.

That's it. If the sun were the size of Peoria, it would be a neutron star. And it might give off gamma rays.

Science is really easy when you have a clear-thinking writer to explain it to you.

Sick Mouse (Pat. Pending)

Animal welfare organizations from 12 European countries are campaigning against the Harvard mouse.

Some definitions may be needed here.

Animal welfare organizations are not groups dedicated to socialized government programs like Aid to Dependent Kittens or Dog Food Stamps or subsidized bird house rentals. Their mission is to protect innocent critters from being rendered into things like medical experiments, fur coats or meat loaf.

And the Harvard mouse is not an animated Disney employee starring in "Mickey Gets His MBA." It is a breed of genetically-altered mouse that biologists have engineered so that it will inevitably develop cancer.

Harvard University made both patent history and genetic history by getting a patent on a living, breathing (and eventually suffering) animal, both in this country and from the European Patent Office headquartered in Germany. The animal protectors don't like that.

Messing with life in the laboratory is not a new cause of outrage. Mary Shelley dredged up the issue very juicily way back in 1818 when she wrote her novel about Dr. Frankenstein.

Unfortunately, Frankenstein didn't get a patent on the chap he created. His monster seems to be in the public domain, and anybody who wants to can assemble a similar monster if he can get together the parts. Or he can make a movie about the monster, which is easier, a lot safer and probably more profitable.

In this post-Frankenstein era, it's interesting how smoothly we slide into acceptance of somebody creating an animal and getting a patent on it.

Fiction on the subject, from Mrs. Shelley to H. P. Lovecraft to second rate horror films, often insists that only evil can come from trying to create life in a laboratory, and thus usurping God's prerogative. Even an Ivy League laboratory.

A spokesperson for the coalition of European animal welfare activists was quoted as saying, "We believe it's inherently contrary to morality to create an animal with the clear intention that it should suffer and die."

Isn't that the way God arranged his creating, too? Do the animal advocates feel that if a scientist can create and patent an organism that never suffers and never dies, then it's all right?

If scientists can now create life, atheists will undoubtedly ballyhoo it as proof that no higher power was needed to create life in the first place. What it may actually prove is that a creator of superior intelligence, human in this case, definitely is needed. If a living thing pops up spontaneously in a petri dish on the back shelf of the lab when nobody is looking, that will be proof that life can get jump-started without a creator.

For a confused layperson, these questions linger:

If the folks at Harvard can incorporate a gene into a mouse's genetic structure that makes it susceptible to cancer, how about whipping up a gene that makes its owner unsusceptible to cancer?

And, if it's so easy to give mice and rats fatal diseases in a laboratory, then why don't the scientists mix together a big batch of all the stuff that causes cancer in rats, dump it down the sewers in all our major cities, and wipe out the obnoxious beasts?

Soon, before somebody takes out a patent on them.

Attack of the Giant Mushroom

Fungus lovers everywhere were impressed when some scientists announced that they have discovered a 100-ton, 1,500-year-old fungus lurking under 37 acres of a state forest in Iron County, Michigan.

If Rod Serling had written a script about the discovery of a 37-acre fungus, television viewers would have said he had gone too far and changed the channel to something more realistic, like Francis the Talking Mule.

Yet a real-life giant fungus has spread out underground and poked up little clumps of itself here and there. Campers in the state forest just thought they were seeing ordinary clumps of Honey Mushrooms.

But a research team was hired by the United States Navy to study the area. In 1988, the biologists took samples of genetic material from the mushroom patches over a five acre site.

They analyzed the genetic material of the fungus, which they call Armillaria bulbosa because scientists like to think up complicated names for things. And they found that all the samples were genetically identical.

All biologists know that this is scientifically impossible, at least until another biologist discovers that it's not. The only conclusion was that all the mushrooms were part of the same organism.

So the biologists kept going, through 1989 and 1990, sampling fungus genes over a wider and wider area, and decided that the vast underground fungus was silently lolling there beneath the oaks and maples, shaped like a triangle about 2,000 feet to the side.

How did they estimate that the mighty mushroom is 1,500 years old? Easy. Armillaria bulbosa grows by putting out thin tubes, and the tubes grow about eight inches a year.

But wait a minute. Why was the Navy paying biologists to study a forest in Michigan? Because 45 miles away they have built a communication system for nuclear submarines, called Project ELF.

ELF stands for "extremely low frequencies." The scientists were studying the environmental impact of waves from the humongous ELF antenna.

The reports about the discovery of the fungus quoted one of the scientists as saying, "The Navy's communication system is in no way related to the size of the fungus we have found."

That denial reveals that he must have thought of the possibility that (a little Twilight Zone music, please) the low frequency waves given off by the submarine communications system could have made the fungus tendrils grow faster than eight inches a year. Suppose it's only five years old, and growing 200 feet a year?

People in upper Michigan have been fighting Project ELF for years. There was 80 percent opposition in two referenda in 1976, and President Carter withdrew support. ELF was redesigned and pushed through by the Reagan and Bush administrations. The plan was for an antenna 56 miles long.

There are scientists who say that extremely low frequency waves can affect the growth of cells and cause other damage to organisms, and there are those who say ELF waves are perfectly safe for human, beast and fungus. The ones who say they are safe are the ones who work for the folks who want to put up ELF-emitting equipment.

Meanwhile, a giant fungus is growing under a forest in Michigan.

Where is Rod Serling when we need him?

Science Proveth That Thy Days Grow Longer

Lots of things get blamed on middle age– an age named after that fact that it's when you start to grow a larger middle.

Middle age, of course, is 35. People who are that age don't like to hear such a suggestion, but the Bible says that the days of our years are three score and 10, and the middle of three score and 10 is a score and a half plus five, which is 35.

One of the feelings that often assaults the hardening brains of post-35 people is that days are getting longer.

Here's good news for them. It isn't middle age. Days really are longer than they used to be. Some scientists have announced it.

Scientists don't have the depth of authority of the above-quoted Bible, and nobody ever translates their pronouncements into pleasant Elizabethan English so they can say things like "The days of the earth increaseth in length, that thou mayest rejoice in it."

But an astronomer named Kevin Pang and his associates at NASA's Jet Propulsion Laboratory in Pasadena, Cal., claim to have proved that the earth's rotation has slowed down over the past 3,200 years.

The Pang team figured this out by studying some ancient shoulder blades of oxen.

It seems that long ago, some folks in Anyang, China, used to keep records of things by scratching on shoulder blades of oxen (after the oxen were decently deceased, of course, and the blades removed.)

They probably wrote on the shoulder blades of oxen because there wasn't any paper and pencil handy. It's a familiar problem. It happens in our house when the telephone rings and somebody wants to leave a message. If there were an old shoulder blade on the end table at one of those moments, it would be written on.

Some ancient Chinese jotted down on oxen bones the exact time of five eclipses of the sun between 1226 and 1161 B.C. They also recorded where the shadow of the moon fell in Anyang during the eclipses.

Pang and friends, using oxen shoulder blades and computers, figured out from the ox-bone data that the earth's rotation has indeed slowed down. A day was 47 thousandths of a second shorter in 1200 B.C. than it was today, give or take a fortnight.

What's that you say, you people who have passed the age of a score and a half plus five? The length of days seems to have increased a bit more than that? And lately your life seems to be made up of shorter weeks composed of longer days?

Well, maybe it is middle age after all. The scientists will have to dig up another set of oxen shoulder blades and check it out.

If your own shoulder blades ache a little after one of those longer days, that could be middle age, too. Sorry.

Facts (Probably) About Dinosaurs

Dinosaurs are a big item with kids these days. I perused an 18-page childrens' booklet on the subject that was full of color drawings of mighty lizards gallumphing around, or of their bones standing still.

The text was minimal and mostly captions. The introduction stated very positively that dinosaurs lived on this earth for more than 160 million years, that the earliest ones lived more than 225 million years ago and the last ones died about 65 million years ago. It told about dinosaurs that ate other animals and dinosaurs that ate vegetation.

On page three, the book warned that "Newspaper articles, popular books, and movies about dinosaurs are often filled with mistakes." This happens, it said, because "they may fail to check with scientists to find out what the real facts are."

I started to read, looking forward to getting some of that real, factual saurian information.

But the rest of the book was a bit hesitant about the promised scientific facts.

The word "probably" was used 14 times. The phrase "may have" appeared 10 times. There were a combined total of 16 uses of "might have", "might have been", "might be", "may be", "might" or "could have." There were also a "seems likely", a "seems to", an "it is possible", an "as far as we know" and a "this may mean".

It must be nice to be a scientist and be able to use qualifiers like that when you present facts to the world.

A paleontologist wouldn't last long in the newspaper business. I began picturing the reaction of some city editors I've worked for, if I turned in a news story written like the dinosaur book:

"What may have been a man was probably injured in what might have been an accident, probably yesterday, when his car could have run off what might be Main st. and probably struck what it is possible was a tree. As far as we know, police said it seems likely he could have been John Jones, might be 49 and probably lives on what seems to be Elm st."

That wouldn't hack it in journalism, but in paleontology it might be okay.

This may mean that a scientist probably needs to have a lot of faith, since there is often so much that is not known about absolutely true facts.

An astronomer from Pennsylvania State University revealed the dilemma recently when discussing black holes.

Black holes demand even more faith than dinosaurs, because scientists at least have some bones and footprints from dinosaurs. Black holes in space are theoretical, although some astronomers have claimed that they probably have detected what it seems likely may be black holes, off in the cosmos somewhere.

There are some astronomers who can't quite accept the idea of black holes, despite the evidence from such authorities as Isaac Newton, Albert Einstein, Stephen Hawking and Jean-Luc Piccard.

And the Penn State astronomer was quoted as saying about black holes: "I'm more comfortable with a swarm of neutron stars, because I can understand neutron stars."

Well, I'm more comfortable with cocker spaniels than with tyrannosaurs, so I know how he feels.

What's New in the Universe

Two teams of what newspaper reports called distinguished astronomers, working independently, recently announced the most accurate estimates yet of the age of the universe. Both concluded that the universe is younger and smaller than astronomers, even undistinguished ones, previously thought.

This is good news. The whole purpose of science is for dedicated experimenters, observers and analyzers to disprove the theories the last batch of experts proclaimed.

Scientists in various eras often wandered around telling anyone who would listen that the world is flat, there are 92 elements or the universe is 20 billion years old.

Then, along came spoilsports who discovered the western hemisphere, a whole bunch of extra elements, and now, new data which indicate that the universe is a mere seven billion years old.

The separate studies were done by teams of astronomers at Indiana University and Harvard University. Newspaper articles describe them as teams, because reporters see this aspect of science as a kind of college sport. Teams whose discoveries beat old theories are champions.

Your typical scientist can handle this sort of thing. Rethinking something when new data infect it is what scientists do for a living.

Newspaper writers have a harder time with it. They naively believe in the existence of facts, and don't like to see details altered after they've been in print.

So newspersons covering the latest measurement of the universe write about the scientific world being startled by challenges to long-held assumptions, and give the impression that astronomers may soon be leaping off the domes of their observatories in frustration because somebody has recalculated Hubble's Constant, whatever that is, and revised the age of the universe.

Reporters seemed particularly intrigued that the recent universe-revisers maintain that the oldest stars and galaxies in the universe are still about 16 billion years old, even though they've decided that the universe itself is maybe half that age.

The papers quote a Harvard astronomer that "we have a problem," and a NASA astronomer that "there is something profound going on."

Having a universe that is younger than some of the material in it will certainly lead to a few pleasant seminars and some dense treatises with many footnotes.

A universe that is newer than its contents doesn't bother me so much. The material my house is made of is older than the house, and the material I'm made of is older than I am, so why shouldn't the stars be older than the universe?

I am confident that the astronomers will all buckle down and study the new information, and will come up with a theory explaining the paradox. If they're lucky, they will announce their conclusions well before the time that some other scientists publish some other new figures that seem to change everything again.

Meanwhile, there are surely clumps of Fundamentalist theologians and Creation Scientists here and there who are sitting around snickering as they read about the astronomers' new ambiguity.

They thought all along that "there is something very profound going on," but they are convinced that the book of Genesis covers the subject.

Washington
(D. C., Not George)

Our nation's capital was assembled in a 63-square-mile swamp between 1790 and 1800, an odd location for a swamp. During the War of 1812, the British army burned down all of its major structures except Dolley Madison, but it was rebuilt and now has a population of 600,000, eight percent unemployed not counting Congress. Extremely governmental things tend to happen there.

The Napping of the President

A Washington reporter for a big metropolitan daily newspaper wrote an article about what he obviously feels is one of the better attributes of President Clinton: He is good at taking naps.

This, the reporter explained, keeps the president rested and alert and makes him more effective.

I don't know how long this reporter has been covering the goings on in the District of Calamity. Maybe before the Clinton administration started administering, he was on the lacrosse beat or covered truck farming or wrote the "Deaths Elsewhere" part of the obituary page.

But if he has been hanging around D. C. since the good old days of the Eighties, when the federal budget was under a trillion dollars and the income tax laws had not yet been simplified to the point that we couldn't understand them, he might remember another president who took naps.

That president's name was Ronald Reagan. And when he took naps, the Washington news writers proclaimed with loud hoo-hawing that this was a sign of near incompetence and approaching senility.

The last time I remember a president being praised for taking naps, it was John F. Kennedy.

There is a suspicion here that your typical Washington newshawk believes that when a Democrat takes a nap he is rejuvenating his creative juices, but when a Republican nods off he is exhibiting signs of flabby acumen.

This thought will not surprise the large number of conservatives who subscribe to the idea that most newspaper writers and editors are wild-eyed leftwingers who would find truth and beauty in any action of a Democrat president, from solving the Middle East crisis to nose-picking.

Fortunately for democracy, journalism and similar bastions of fair play, the conservative carpers are neatly counterbalanced by the legions of liberals who believe that all newspaper publishers are hard-eyed right-wingers, sitting behind their big desks and big cigars as they order their staffs to support Republican plots to suppress the poor and downtrodden.

The sad truth is that newspaper persons are merely normal human beings (with a few exceptions I decline to identify at this time.)

That means that professional news purveyors have, randomly distributed among them, all the varieties of prejudices and opinions that prevail among the general population.

It also means that no matter how hard they may try to be objective, some of their private feelings may sift into their reportorial judgment.

And it further means that there are an unpleasant few who don't even try to be objective.

So we have to be tolerant of the writer who considers President Clinton's frequent dozing a virtue, after others of the capital's press corps proclaimed President Reagan's catnaps laughable.

If the writer did let his own opinions creep into his evaluation of White House napping, maybe it was because he missed some sleep himself.

For all reporters assigned to evaluate the highly-charged Washington political landscape, I recommend an occasional nap in the office, as relief from the rigors of those long, hard days full of interviewing highly placed sources who asked that their names not be used.

Farmers Down, Astronauts Up

A business magazine reported in mid-1992 that the number of farmers in the United States has been declining by two percent a year, but the number of employees of the U.S. Department of Agriculture keeps going up.

At that moment, there were 3,199,000 farmers and 122,062 USDA employees.

If the average rates of decreasing farmers and increasing USDA workers stay on the same curves as the previous 60 years, the report said, by the year 2059 there will be one USDA employee for every farmer.

I don't know where the figures came from, but probably the farmers were counted by the USDA. I can't guess who counts USDA employees. I'm sure it's not farmers; they're too busy.

When the numbers finally equal out in 2059, it will be easy for the USDA people to count the farmers. Each government worker can just count one farmer.

It will be very convenient for every farmer to have his own assigned government employee. Maybe the government people can close down the offices in Washington and here and there, saving the taxpayers a lot of money, and each one can move in with the designated farmer.

The resident USDA operative can take care of all the paperwork that the department has created for farmers down through the years, and in odd moments can help shovel out the barn, a roughly equivalent procedure.

Government agencies do tend to grow without much relationship to the folks they're agenting for.

There are, for instance, 535 members of Congress. In 1992, they were supported by 20,265 employees.

Compare that to 1964. That year was carefully chosen for this research because it was the year of the oldest almanac gathering dust in the office, and I'm not going to do anything radical like going to a library.

In 1964, there were 535 members of Congress, supported by 8,132 employees.

In other words, 28 years B. C. (Before Clinton) there were 15 employees for every Congressman, and by the days of George Bush there were 37.

If that growth rate continues, in 2059 there will be approximately the same number of Congressional employees as there are farmers and employees of the Department of Agriculture.

On the other hand, in 1964 NASA had 30 astronauts and 29,934 employees. By 1992 there were 97 astronauts and only 25,529 employees.

Of course, it's a lot easier to take care of outer space than farms. Nothing in outer space has to be fed, milked, herded, butchered, plucked, plowed, planted, fertilized, reaped, fenced or mortgaged, and no coop-scraping or stable-shoveling is needed. At least, not that I know of.

And astronauts must be easier to take care of than Congressmen. In orbit, nobody has to please constituents, coax votes, write overdrawn checks, harass female visitors, do lunch with lobbyists, embarrass Supreme Court nominees, make windy speeches, show off for C-Span or even pass occasional laws.

But pro-rating those growth rates again, by the time there are equal numbers of farmers, USDA employees and

Congressional employees, there will be almost as many astronauts as there are Congressmen.

Today's homework problem: In how many years will there be more astronauts than farmers?

Welcome to the Senate, Girls

Now that the United States Senate has more women members than ever before, let us remember the roses Joe Biden sent Barbara Boxer.

Rep. Barbara Boxer (D-Cal) is one of the new female Senators. She was one of the seven members of the House of Representatives who marched on the Senate in October of 1991 to demand that the Judiciary Committee delay its vote on the appointment of Clarence Thomas to the Supreme Court until it heard testimony from Anita Hill.

Anyone who needs an explanation of the Hill-Thomas uproar is excused at this point.

The Judiciary Committee's performance in the roasting of Ms. Hill and Justice Thomas is widely credited with getting a bunch of female Senators elected. The committee, sensitive to criticism that it is an all-male organism (and probably somewhat rattled to find itself being sensitive to anything other than party politics) naturally felt its collective consciousness raised to the point that the members sighed something along the lines of, "Guess we oughta let some broads in."

So when Rep. Boxer won the Democratic Senate primary in California, the chairman of the Judiciary boys, Sen. Joseph R. Biden, Jr. (D-Del) wrote her a note, vaguely tongue-in-cheek, saying "Welcome to the Senate Judiciary Committee."

The note was accompanied by a dozen red roses.

If I were a female Senatorial candidate at that point, I would have run screaming into the streets, flinging roses wildly at the heavens and asking, "What do we have to do to get through to these guys?"

This outburst would have been triggered by the following thoughts:

1. There is no record of Sen. Biden ever sending roses with a communication to any male politician.

2. Running for Senate is not equivalent to running for Homecoming Queen.

3. Installing a token woman on the Judiciary Committee is not likely to erase the memory of the smirking circus Justice Thomas and Ms. Hill were compelled to star in.

4. Nor will it alter anyone's image of some members of the committee, like Sen. Kennedy's sorry record in dealing with women or Sen. Thurmond's ancient stances on civil rights.

Sen. Biden and some other Senators apparently found it odd that their new female colleagues weren't panting eagerly to join the jolly crew of the Judiciary Committee, preferring committees like Appropriations, or those that deal with banking, commerce, housing, and other heavy stuff.

Golly. Just like new male Senators. Who would have guessed?

All along, we masculine members of the populace thought that when enough women mysteriously forsook their aprons and beauty parlor appointments to become Senators, the Congress would have to create some new committees for them, like the Select Committee on Cooking, Cleaning and Laundry.

But then, the little ladies always were good at handling the household money; what's the harm in letting a gal be on the Appropriations Committee, fellas?

What kind of corsage did the boys buy Barbara for her first day on the job?

The Political Joke is On Us

Farmers in Bangalore, India, staged a protest against some unpopular local government policies. For two hours, 20,000 farmers stood in front of the government offices and laughed. There were 2,000 policemen on hand to keep order, but the cops didn't do anything. The police commissioner ruled that there is no law against laughing.

The same would be true in this country. As everyone knows, the Next-to-the-Last Amendment clearly states that the government shall make no law respecting the right of the people to peaceably assemble, take a good look at the government and then laugh their heads off.

Laughing at the government is a time-honored democratic tradition.

Socrates and Plato probably spent a lot of time laughing while chatting about what was wrong with the government. Plato called democracy "a charming form of government, full of variety and disorder."

From "Joe Miller's Jests" published in England in 1739 to nearly forgotten 19th century American writers like Petroleum V. Nasby and Artemus Ward, humorists have led the citizens in laughing at the government. In our time, we've had commentators like Will Rogers, Mort Sahl and Bob Hope.

During the last presidential primaries, a research organization kept track of jokes told about the candidates by Johnny Carson, Jay Leno and David Letterman on late night television. The score for the first 11 weeks of the year was George Bush, 97 jokes; Bill Clinton, 46; Pat Buchanan, 35; Paul Tsongas, 28, and Jerry Brown, 26. That was 232 jokes in 165 programs.

The amount of laughter candidates can generate suggests a solution to the voters who complain that they don't like any of the presidential contenders. Instead of voting, they should all gather outside their polling places on election day and laugh.

Most normal people don't like to be laughed at, and that possibly includes a few politicians. Maybe our leaders would start listening to the citizens if instead of petitioning, writing letters and demonstrating, we publicly laughed at them. Maybe people who show up to protest in the meetings of Congress, state legislatures, City Councils, county commissioners or township supervisors should not bother booing, chanting, applauding, making speeches or carrying signs. Maybe they should stand there and laugh, chuckle, giggle, chortle, snicker, hoot, guffaw, howl, cackle, titter, roar, slap their thighs and hold their sides.

But while laughing at the politicians, we have to remember the sad truth: the joke is on us.

Department of Strange Information

Strange information comes out of Washington, D. C. regularly. It may be that every federal agency has one or two trained professionals designated Strange Information Officers, who are in charge of issuing strange information to the news media.

One strange news item had to do with the Treasury Department's handling of torn currency.

It said that if a citizen turns in three-fifths or more of a bill, the Treasury will give him or her the full face value. For less than three fifths, it will give only half the value.

This seems to tell us that if I take a $100 bill and carefully tear it into three fifths and two fifths, the Treasury will pay me $100 for the big piece and $50 for the small piece.

I'm considering going into bill-tearing as a full time occupation. The profit for the amount of labor involved is impressive.

From the Strange Information Department of the Census Bureau comes the announcement that in more than 2,000 cities, counties, towns and other incorporated localities, minorities are now in the majority.

Minorities make up the majority in six of the eight largest American cities, the Census Bureau reports with a straight face. In Detroit, 80 percent of the citizens are minorities.

The Censusers classify African Americans, Asians, Pacific Islanders, American Indians, Inuits and Aleuts as racial minorities. Hispanics slip into the minority list also. Non-Hispanic whites are considered to be the majority.

In one locality out of 24, the federal nose counters maintain, the minority population is bigger than the majority.

The dictionary, of course, says a majority is the greatest part of a group; a minority is the smallest part. Only a federal agency could create a system where the smallest part of something is bigger than the biggest part.

From the Bureau of Labor Statistics, which often functions as a Strange Information source in toto, we learn that 500,000 clerical and technical jobs were eliminated in 1992.

But the good news was that employment increased in some businesses. The biggest new job boom was in the movie production industry, where employment increased 28.5 percent since 1988.

By comparison, the health care and computer industries, which one might expect to be growing faster than the craft of photographing Sharon Stone's upper thighs or the rampages of artificial dinosaurs, increased only about 16 percent in the same period.

The labor statisticers seem to have found lots of job growth in some parts of the economy. The Walt Disney Co. added 19,000 new workers since 1988.

In that same four-year statistical chunk, the number of writers, artists and musicians increased 20 percent. Employment by museums, civic and cultural organizations went up nearly 10 percent.

The Clinton administration could really make the economy

look good if it would have the Census Bureau declare film makers, writers, artists, musicians, museum workers and Mickey Mouse impersonators to be majorities. Then the government could announce huge increases in employment among a majority of workers.

Self-employed currency-tearers might become a growing category, too.

Writings Written About Writing

If a writer can't write about writing, what can he write about? Right?

How to Write News Articles

There are little tricks in every profession. For those of you who are considering journalism as a career, because you aren't agile enough to be a burglar and sing too clearly to be a rock star, here are some things you should know about news writing.

If you want to write like a professional, remember that people never just cry. They weep openly. Notice reports of any sad event. They never say, "Mrs. Schnuffler cried." It's always, "Mrs. Schnuffler wept openly."

When somebody is assaulted, be sure to use the phrase "brutally beaten." If you should write that someone was beaten badly or beaten hard, or even viciously beaten, it's a giveaway that you aren't a seasoned reporter.

When someone is shot, be sure to mention that it was a senseless shooting. Otherwise, readers might get the impression that it was sensible.

Victims of senseless shootings, every serious news writer knows, are often innocent bystanders. Never call them simply bystanders. All bystanders are innocent ones.

And when a senseless shooting takes place, what do the police do? (a) Look for clues. (b) Comb the area for clues.

If you answered (b), you have the makings of a news writer. It's all in knowing the correct terminology. Always remember: salaries, taxes and transit fares are never raised; they are hiked. Heavy rains are downpours; really heavy rains are torrential downpours. And what does heavy snow do? It blankets the area.

When it's hot, don't forget to mention that the mercury soared. (Sometimes it climbs, but soaring is preferred by discriminating journalists).

When police cars chase non-police cars, be sure to point out that the chase was high-speed. If you don't, the reader will assume that the officers and the suspects were both doing 27 miles per hour.

And when a car runs off a curve, the correct phrase is "the car failed to negotiate the curve." If an embankment adjoins the non-negotiable curve, the car plunges down it. Cars rarely just fall.

Some news writing rules apply specifically to television news. On TV, starting a report with "ironically" is highly desirable, whether or not there is anything ironic forthcoming. Also, as you may have noticed, it is compulsory to use the word "tragedy" at least once in every telecast.

Since the television industry, when not reporting news, attempts to be an entertainment medium, TV news writers like to compare real live events with titles of well-known movies whenever possible. For example:

If a child is discovered living on cat food for a week while his parents are spelunking in the Verkhoyansk Mountains, always begin the script by announcing, "Another case of Home Alone." If a woman fills her married boyfriend's carcass with 20 rounds from her favorite Ingram M-11 Machine Pistol, don't fail to call it a Fatal Attraction case.

It's knowing the little tricks like these that makes a news writer produce reports just like all the other writers. And we all aspire to that.

How to Write News of Fires

You, too, can learn the easy art of newswriting. All you need is to master a few simple concepts and you can write for newspapers, radio or television.

Today's lesson: Things You Need to Know to Write About Fires.

There are several kinds of fires. There are fires, blazes and (if they're big enough) infernos and even conflagrations.

Blazes can be stubborn or intense. A newsperson never calls a fire stubborn; it's always a stubborn blaze. The same goes for intense. Blazes are often spectacular. A spectacular blaze is more common than a mere spectacular fire.

Many fires are suspicious fires. More elegantly put, they are of suspicious origin. Be sure to mention that the cause is under investigation. Never describe a fire as being unsuspicious.

Fires rarely just start; they break out, or erupt.

Fires, once they erupt or break out, burn out of control. They do this until firefighters get the stubborn blaze under control. Firefighters accomplish this by pouring streams of water on the flames.

Fires at which more than one alarm is sounded rage out of control. Smaller fires don't rage.

Buildings that catch fire are often engulfed in flames. When flames are not engulfing, they most often leap into the air. Some flames leap hundreds of feet into the air.

Most fires produce smoke. There are various kinds of smoke. There is dense smoke, acrid smoke, thick smoke, thick black smoke and dense acrid smoke. The basic configuration of smoke is a column. Columns of smoke rise in the air above fires. Dense columns of smoke can usually be seen; be sure to mention how far they can be seen. Typically, a dense column of smoke can be seen for miles.

Flames that leap hundreds of feet in the air can also be seen for miles, especially if associated with a spectacular blaze.

Columns of smoke and flames can sometimes be seen in nearby communities. Firefighters from nearby communities often come to help local firefighters battle the blaze, especially the stubborn variety.

Several things can hamper firefighters while they pour streams of water on a stubborn blaze. A good newswriter should be sure to mention any hampering that is going on. High winds can hamper firefighters. So can intense heat, or intense cold. (If the intense cold is below 32 degrees Fahrenheit, don't fail to work in the phrase "subfreezing temperatures" in the hampering section). Dense smoke can do the trick, and dense, acrid smoke is a nifty hamperer.

When writing about a fire, never omit the word "tragic" or "tragedy", especially in a television news script. No newscast is considered complete without the word "tragedy" being used at least once.

Buildings are damaged by fires. If they are badly damaged, they are said to be gutted. "Fire Guts Building" is a popular headline because "guts" fits so much better than "destroys the interior of."

This is all you need to know to write news articles about fires. Avoid using any words that are more descriptive or less trite than those mentioned above, and you will go far in the fire reporting business.

When Names Become Words

The word "eponymous" has become a fad recently, popping up in newspaper and magazine articles.

An eponym, the various dictionaries agree, is a proper name that has become a word in everyday language.

Writers treat an unusual word the way little kids treat an empty can in the street; when they discover it, they start kicking it around.

The other day a newspaper article called Trump's Castle eponymous, because it was named after Donald Trump, and a television columnist wrote about "the eponymous Tracey Ullman Show." That kind of usage is common, but it isn't right.

Neither Trump nor Ullman are part of the English language. They aren't eponymous.

When you call a guy a casanova because he chases women like the late Giovanni Casanova, that's an eponym. If people begin calling a guy a trump because he is a rich man's son who becomes famous by marrying assorted blondes and spending millions building skyscrapers and casinos, then Trump will be eponymous.

There are a lot of dandy genuine eponyms in the world. A baby born by caesarean is born the same way Julius Caesar was born in 102 B.C., although it probably didn't cost his parents DCCLXIII dollars a day for a hospital bed, the way it might these days.

The derby hat and the horse races called derbies are eponymous. They were named for the 12th Earl of Derby, who invented both of them. His real name was Edward Stanley, and if he hadn't been an earl, we might be watching the Kentucky Stanley on television every May.

And aren't you glad that John Montagu became the fourth Earl of Sandwich? You'd feel pretty silly ordering a ham montagu on rye down at the deli.

Many inventions have become eponymous. They took the name of the inventor. Louis Braille devised a system of writing for the blind. Julius Leotard created a comfortable garment for dancers. Dr. Joseph Guillotine invented what he claimed was a more humane method of execution than hanging.

The stories of why some names became words aren't always clear. Old Sam Maverick of Texas either let his calves run around unbranded and other ranchers grabbed them, or grabbed other people's stray calves and put his own brand on them, depending on which Texan tells the story. But a maverick is now an ornery runaway, either way.

And Etienne de Silhouette, a French finance minister in 1757, either advocated the economy of buying paper cut-outs instead of expensive portraits, or was such a lousy finance minister that he seemed like a paper cut-out himself, according to which Frenchman tells the story.

Who knows what names might become eponyms? If London cops are called bobbies after Sir Robert Peel, maybe someday Philadelphia cops will be called rizzos. Maybe to lead a city to the brink of bankruptcy will become known as gooding the city, and to bail the city out again will be to rendell it.

Maybe someday people will talk about a future president who nixoned or a preacher who bakkered, of an army that schwarzkopfed the enemy or a singer who milli-vanillied a record. To reform a system of government will be to gorby it, and if there really is a new world order it will be said that the world has been bushed. Maybe there will be a health insurance system called Hillarycare.

Meanwhile, newspaper writers should move on to another fad word. They've polished off eponymous.

Invasion of the Brackets

Brackets are moving in on us. I don't know where they come from, but more and more brackets are creeping into the quotations in newspaper articles.

There doesn't seem to be a rational explanation of the phenomenon. It used to be that writers just plain quoted people's real statements.

But now brackets mysteriously pop in and replace words, so readers can only guess what was actually said.

I ignored the bracket plague for a while. Then it started to bother me, so I decided to clip a few examples from the big daily newspapers that have been invaded by the brackets.

Here are some troubling results of my bracket survey: A comedian was quoted as having said, "Okay, maybe [I'll] be in a club and someone tells a joke and [I] don't laugh at it." Why the brackets? What did he really say if he didn't say "I'll" and "I"?

Another actual bracket-besmirched quote from a newspaper: "Everybody seemed to be making the adjustment pretty good. For some reason, he [didn't]." What could the man have said that those sneaky brackets felt compelled to replace?

Or try this one: "He seemed very much more at ease and in a [better] frame of mind than I've seen him in a long time." If "better" isn't what the man said, what was the word?

And here's a maddening bracketization: A jockey was talking about a horse. "Since the first time I rode him," the sportswriter quoted the jockey, "he"s an eighth-of-a-mile [faster]." Why is "faster" in brackets? Is it replacing the word the guy really used? If so, what could he have said? Was the horse an eighth-of-a-mile longer? An eighth-of-a-mile away? An eighth-of-a-mile from Coon Rapids, Minnesota?

Also, in an article mentioning the London street called Bishopsgate, a man was quoted as citing "one building [on] Bishopsgate."

What other word could he have used but "on", that would make a pair of explanatory brackets eagerly leap into the sentence? Maybe some quaint British expression unfamiliar to Yankees like us?

Yet another bracket manifestation appeared in the quoted statement, "[President] Clinton promised not to raise taxes."

Presumably, the brackets are trying to prevent us from confusing [President] Clinton with [County Commissioner Fillmore T.] Clinton, who has proposed a tax increase in Mulespit County, Missouri.

There must be a reason that brackets are suddenly intruding

on our printed material, arrogantly replacing words without leaving us a clue to the real meanings. Maybe it's some kind of plot. Who could be behind it? It can't be the Russians; they're on our side now. It can't be Middle East terrorists, or the brackets would be wired with plastic explosives. Maybe the Japanese are dumping low-priced brackets on the American market to undercut our bracket industry.

Whatever is [going] on with brackets, it annoys [me] a little.

Pre-Programmed Media Bias

An advertisement for a book promises that it exposes a long list of television's conservative political commentators "whose opinions are pre-programmed to fit the needs of the corporations that own the airwaves, or purchase air time."

Those commentators would probably say that the author of the book is one of those ultra liberal writers whose opinions are preprogrammed to fit the needs of the world marxists who seek to undermine the American way of life.

True believers of the extreme left and the extreme right have at least one thing in common: neither can conceive of any honest person disagreeing with their point of view.

So, if they come upon an apparently intelligent believer at the opposite extreme, the only conclusion they can reach is that the opponent's thoughts are being controlled by some insidious outside force.

The left-wing believers can explain patiently their absolute knowledge that Wall Street, the big corporations and limo-riding, nanny-hiring cigar-smokers in expensive suits totally control the conservative news media.

And the right-wing believers can explain patiently their absolute knowledge that commie-hugging, fuzzy-thinking, loose-living subversives totally infest the liberal news media.

It must be confusing for the extreme right media-exposers these days.

There was a time when they could reveal the truth very simply: the pinkos took their orders directly from Moscow. But world communism seems to be in disarray right now, and hardly able to control itself, much less the American news media. The conservatives will have to search for new culprits.

Meanwhile, the lucky media exposers on the extreme left can still find the corporations and the millionaires lurking in the bushes outside the offices of the news media, whispering their foul instructions.

But be assured that the whiners on the right will regroup soon and find the proper villain to blame for the fact that the media don't always report things the way the whiners think well-behaved media should.

Also, experience makes me confident that the musings you are reading at this moment will infuriate dwellers at each extreme.

Any piece of writing that intimates that both political extremes may be equally misguided inevitably is received the same way by both: as support of "their" lies and an attack on "our" privately-owned truth.

One of the modest delights of newspaper columnizing is receiving two letters about the same piece of writing, one claiming it's the work of a Limbaugh-loving capitalist flunky, and the other branding it the product of a card-carrying ADA and ACLU red.

Curiously, letter writers from the two extremes never claim they detect bias toward their cause. If a writer tries to give two sides of a story, he will be denounced by the proponents of Side A for including Side B, but not praised for presenting A. And vice versa.

That's what we writers get for allowing ourselves to be pre-programmed by Wall Street and the Kremlin simultaneously.

Where Ideas Come From

One of the questions that regular readers frequently ask writers of newspaper columns is, "Where do you get your ideas for column subjects?"

Another question frequently asked by regular readers is, "Are you under the care of a mental health professional at this time?"

Today, we shall consider the first question.

It must be pointed out that many readers who ask where ideas originate immediately follow the question with suggestions for topics.

These suggestions typically involve such vibrant subjects as an uncle who can play two harmonicas simultaneously, a neighborhood dry cleaner celebrating his 37th anniversary in business, a six-year-old baton twirler who lives down the block and has earned 14 trophies, a dog that howls in accompaniment of Andy Williams records, or an exploration of the place of current phenomenological thinking in Judeo-Christian considerations of Roger Penrose's cosmologic views.

Suggestions, as you can see, are always helpful.

The truth is that once people find out you are writing this type of newspaper essay on a regular basis, they are compelled to offer suggestions. They can't help themselves.

People are seized with the compulsion to give writers ideas in the same way that dogs are compelled to snarl at letter carriers; teenagers in open cars are compelled to turn up the radio so loud that the throbs of the bass leave regular indentations in the road paving; comedians are compelled to make jokes about Vice Presidents; television news anchors are compelled to use the word "tragedy"; supermarket clerks are compelled to insist that you have a nice day; fish got to swim, birds got to fly, and so forth.

Writers get used to it.

Once, years ago, we were moving into a new house. The

moving van had just left. The telephone installer finished installing and drove off. Only I and Directory Assistance, in all of creation, knew the new number.

Soon, the phone rang. Our first call in our new home was from a guy I never heard of. He said he had once been my grandmother's insurance agent, and he had an idea for a column topic.

So writers get ideas from relatives, friends, friends' friends, friends' relatives, relatives' friends, unrelated (and sometimes unfriendly) readers, and just about anybody who knows that the writer writes.

Sometimes I get ideas myself. I try not to. I hate to disappoint all those other people.

Some suggesters become insistent, and even nasty, if the writer doesn't immediately pronounce the suggestion as immeasurably the best idea since some guy said to Shakespeare, "Geez, Bill, why don't you write something about that Danish prince, what's-his-name?"

Such idea-thrusters demand that the writer sit down at the keyboard immediately and begin rendering the proposed topic into prose fit to be engraved on large stone tablets in a public place.

There is a tested method to discourage the insistent idea hound. Tell him you will consider the topic only in writing; he must sit down and write out the story in full detail.

Request that he work on his idea as hard as he expects you to work on it, and it's unlikely you'll hear from him again.

A Headline Writer Comes Home

Ed sighed wearily as he entered his front door after a hard day at the copy desk of the East Mulespit Daily Fabricator.

"Hi, dear," said his wife, Sue. "You look tired."

"Copy Crunch Hits Desk," said Ed.
"Staff Short."

"Oh, it's terrible that you're so short handed down there," said Sue. "Did you ask the managing editor about the possibility of hiring some other editors, as you said you would?"

"Bid fails; No Aid Due," said Ed.

"Did you bring up the idea that you deserve a salary increase?" Sue asked.

"Boss Nixes Pay Hike; Cites Budget Woes."

"That's too bad, dear," said Sue. "Are you ready for dinner? We're having pork chops and beans."

"Menu Ok'd," Ed replied.
"Spawns Hunger."

"Well, let's eat. You have to drive Junior to his Little League game. I hope the team does better than last week."

"Loss Stuns Locals," said Ed, nibbling a pork chop.
"Rematch Set."

"I still think that Junior was safe on that play at third base," Sue said.

"Coach Assails Refs," Ed said.
"Jr. Vows Come-Back."

"Where is the team in the standings?"

"Close 2nd in Tight Race. Nipped By Foes, Ousted From 1st."

"Try not to be too angry about it," Sue advised. "You wouldn't want to upset my mother when she arrives tomorrow."

Ed looked dismayed.

"Long Visit Mom's Aim?" he asked.

"No," said his wife. "Just for the weekend, to celebrate her birthday."

"Gala Fete Planned?" Ed wanted to know.

"Just a little family get-together," Sue assured him.

"Natal Day Sparks Visit," Ed muttered.
"Kin Seek Free Eats."

Sue pointed to the clock. Ed gulped down his coffee.

"Time Crunch Spurs Pair to Cut Meal,"

he said as he and Junior headed out the door.

"Dad, Son Bid 'Bye to Mrs."

Fashion Statements

These days, people are often identified by their clothing. Businessmen are facetiously called suits, because they wear them. Certain soldiers are called Green Berets, because they wear them. Athletes are called jocks, presumably because of something they wear. That's how important clothing is.

Discussing International Ties

 here was a headline in a newspaper that said, "U. S. to Discuss Ties With Palestinians."

It's about time, I thought, and began to picture what the first meeting would be like.

On the U. S. side of the table would be the usual D. C. types in somber suits, a few of the more daring ones wearing the new double breasted models with pointy lapels that the suit designers have resurrected after studying 1948 photographs. Many would be wearing white shirts; a few, this being a Democrat administration, would have blue button-down oxfords.

All, naturally, would be wearing ties.

Across the table, some Palestinians would be in khakimilitary style jackets with lots of pockets and epaulets. Others would be in robes. Most would be wearing that headgear that looks, to us American chauvinists, like dish towels.

None would be wearing ties.

First there would be small talk, and maybe some smiles and handshakes across the table for the photographers.

Then, the U. S. delegates would get down to business, and discuss ties with the Palestinians.

"I would recommend," the chief American tie negotiator would begin, "a nice paisley print on a 26 ounce silk saglia twill. With a navy background, that would go with almost anything."

The Palestinians would murmur in Arabic and nod approvingly.

"What about an 18-ounce silk repp weave British regimental?" the head of the Palestinian delegation would ask.

"Too traditional," the American would answer. "I'd stay away from Kennedy bar patterns, too. If you're thinking of something geometric, I'd suggest a square neat pattern, maybe in a nice jacquard weave."

And so the discussion would go. Anyone who has seen photos of Mr. Arafat or other Palestinian leaders knows how badly they need to discuss ties with someone who has fashion sense.

Soon, if the discussions go well, Palestinians will all be wearing elegant neckties like civilized men.

The world is, indeed, changing.

And just a few days after that first headline, I saw another one in the newspaper: "Vatican Ready for Ties With Palestinians."

Apparently, the Palestinians are passing along their new-found sophistication.

I began to picture what that first meeting would be like, too.

On the Palestinian side, some delegates would be adorned with jacquard weave ties in refined patterns, tied in windsor knots in the spread collars of their khaki military style jackets with lots of pockets and epaulets. Others would be in robes, but with fashionable ties at the neck. The dish towels would still be there.

The Vatican representatives would include cardinals in red robes with nice little matching skull caps (a much more genteel fashion statement than dish towels), and monsignors in black suits with plain white collars. There wouldn't be a tie in sight.

First there would be small talk, and maybe some smiles and handshakes across the table for the photographers.

Then, the Palestinian delegates would get down to business ....

The Dress Code is Decoded

Herb Lipson, publisher of Philadelphia magazine, in one of his recurring editorials that announce he has detected another aspect of the decay of civilization, described sitting in an elegant and expensive restaurant amid customers wearing polo shirts, T-shirts and other clothing currently referred to as casual attire.

It's called casual because the wearers often look like casualties of something. I have sat in churches, theaters and other formal gathering places, and wondered if some of the people's houses had caught fire just as they were leaving, and they had to dress in a hurry.

I found myself agreeing with Herb Lipson that there is something irritating and dismaying about people dressing for a banquet the same way they would for a picnic.

But I also found myself wondering why it matters. What difference does it make what kind of clothes we wear? What difference does it make whether we wear any clothes at all?

Yet the way we dress remains important to those of us who were brought up when men wore hats with "Stetson" written inside, instead of caps with "Sixers" written outside. And removed said hats indoors.

There was a time when fancy restaurants would refuse to admit a guy without a necktie as severely as they would a guy without trousers.

Today, I suspect, restaurants and other establishments are afraid they might lose a customer by giving him the heave-ho on the grounds of tielessness.

Once, in days of yore when dress codes were enthusiastically enforced, I entered a hotel dining room in the company of a stylish and attractive young woman.

I was wearing an acceptable jacket, but under it was a turtleneck shirt. I am permitted by the rules of society to dress wretchedly, because I am a writer. Our culture indulges artists, musicians and writers (especially poets) in lapses of good taste on the grounds that, if we knew any better, we would be in some respectable line of work like back hoe operator, fish scaler or restroom attendant.

"I'm sorry, sir," said the man at the dining room door, "we can't serve you without a necktie."

But the maitre d' glided up behind him, and scrutinized me and my companion. Your average American maitre d' believes that a middle aged, balding guy accompanying a handsome and well dressed woman must have money. And patrons with money must not be offended.

"He is wearing a necktie," the maitre d' announced, staring at my turtleneck as though willing a Countess Mara original to appear there. "This way, sir."

This may explain to Herb Lipson why folks like to dine graciously while wearing sweatsuits and running shoes. They are proving to themselves that they (and their American Express cards) are so important that they can ignore any dress code. Part of the mystique is to spend a lot of money on clothes that don't seem worth it. The casual dressers would never wear old clothes that are actually old.

Back in the 1960s, when crummy apparel was just coming into its own, a teenaged girl stopped me in a shopping mall and asked me how I got my denim jeans so beautifully worn and faded. She looked a bit shocked when I told her the secret: wear them every weekend for about 15 years.

Of course, I didn't wear jeans to work in those days. I was employed by America's largest evening newspaper, which demanded at least a feeble gesture toward respectable garb. I usually wore a sport jacket and slacks.

Once I was called upon to interview the chief executive of a company that tailored expensive clothing for men. He cast dismayed eyes on my J. C. Penney sport coat, and asked if I owned any of his company's suits. I confessed that at the moment my wardrobe was completely suitless.

"What would you wear if you were going to a banquet?" he asked, his tone puzzled.

"This," I replied.

"What would you wear if you had to sit at the head table at the banquet?"

"This."

"What if you were the speaker?"

"This."

He sighed, and suggested that I stop in at one of his stores, tell them that he sent me, and let them drape me in luxurious acceptability. I never did. Neither did I start feasting at Le Bec Fin in a sweat suit. There is a balance point, even for writers.

Herb Lipson shouldn't be surprised by the popularity of sloppy clothing. It's symbolic that we live in sloppy times: sloppy morals, sloppy education, sloppy government, sloppy environment. Take off your tie, Herb, and join the decline and fall.

Health Care

Health is important because most of us have some, either good or bad. The first two pieces that follow were published before Congress decided that it would be confusing to provide ordinary citizens with as good health insurance as Congresspersons have.

Here's to Your Insured Health

The nation is now watching with wonder and delight as the problem of health care is dissected for later reassembly by the First Ms. (If Bill isn't First Lord, why should Hillary be First Lady?)

She has accepted the person-sized task of figuring out how we ordinary earners can afford to maintain the members of the medical industry in the style to which they are accustomed.

The cost of supporting the laborers in the field of medicine has become very expensive because they insist on finding new ways to cure things, and then demand that we allow them to treat our ailments no matter how many Mercedes the process compels them to buy.

The role of health insurance in this medical care miasma hits home with me quite literally, because home is where I work. Being self-employed, I have to buy my own health insurance.

And I need some kind of health insurance because I am at that inbetween age: too young for Medicare, but too old to stand the strain of being healthy all the time.

Health insurance, like life insurance, is misnamed 180 degrees. Life insurance should probably be called death insurance, and health insurance should be called sickness insurance.

Whatever it is, most of the lucky folks who are privileged to punch a clock every day and take guff from the boss get their health insurance premium paid by the company, and its value is, in essence, money on which they pay no income taxes. The experts estimate that employee benefit health insurance will average $4,400 per employee in value this year.

Those of us cursed to work at home, sleeping late and lolling around with a cup of coffee and doing nothing but writing stuff for a living, have to pay for our own health insurance out of income that is taxed.

There have been hints in the media that Ms. H. Rodham Clinton and her benevolent planners might decide to tax the health insurance benefits lovingly dispensed by the great hearts of corporate America to their faithful toilers. That would be fair.

An alternative, already tried halfheartedly, would be to give the self-employed a tax break on what we have to extract from our feeble bank accounts for health coverage.

Meanwhile, like many other freelancers, I'm taking a chance on the cheapest health insurance feasible.

Under my plan, called Rusty Shield, the cost of anything for which a doctor is likely to charge me is deductible. The plan also entitles the doctor to laugh a lot when he hands me the bill.

On the hospitalization side, I am covered only for afflictions that cause me to be carried into the emergency entrance unconscious or when significant body parts fall off.

I have been looking into the only less expensive plan I've

heard of. It is offered by a witch doctor in Zimbabwe. It's an HMO plan. HMO stands for "Hippopotamus Manure Ointment." It covers everything.

The Health Care Crisis in Action

Every day, the newspapers tell us many cheerful facts about the Health Care Crisis. They have to do this, because on some days there is space left over after including all the available information about figure skater knee smashing, abused wives altering their husbands' anatomy or the amount of blackmail Michael Jackson paid small boys.

Because of the Health Care Crisis, our national leaders worry extensively about people who have no health insurance because they can't afford it.

The leaders never seem to worry about the people who can't afford health insurance, but buy it anyway. These timid souls are afraid that if they acquire pneumonia or bubonic plague or a fractured ischium, some medical practitioner may get wind of it, demand to heal them, and send them a bill equal to the annual salary of a professional basketball center.

So some people who can't afford health insurance pay for it anyway, on the off-chance that an insurance company might actually shell out a small part of the cost of any medical care that is inflicted on them.

After spending money on health insurance, they have to cut back on expenditures for other things, like breakfast, shoes or next month's rent.

Since experts studying the Health Care Crisis seem interested mostly in people who have no health insurance because they can't afford it, the people who can't afford it but have it anyway should consider cancelling their health plans immediately. That way they officially become part of the Health Care Crisis, and have a chance to get some help when our national leaders wave their legislative wands and eliminate the Crisis.

Those who take that risk will have to be careful to avoid accidents, dangerous micro-organisms, or those two most serious of all health threats: Pre-existing Conditions and Preventive Medicine.

Pre-existing Conditions are extremely hard to cure. Insurance companies that don't blanch at paying for medulla oblongata transplants or earlobe replacements shy away from covering Pre-existing Conditions.

Insurers often will pay for Preventive Medicine, however. Preventive Medicine is what doctors call tests. What do tests prevent? They prevent doctors from having to wait until you are really sick to send you bills.

Preventive Medicine works like this: you go to the doctor for hangnail removal. He asks incidentally if everything is okay with your (fill in an embarrassing major organ of your choice here.) You say yes. He suggests a simple new test to check out that organ. You hesitantly agree. You take the test. It hurts a little and costs a little.

The results come back from the laboratory. They are in that scary zone the medical profession calls a Gray Area. But don't worry, there is another test. You take it. It hurts a little more and costs a little more.

The new results come back. Good news, says the doctor. There is nothing wrong with the major organ of your choice.

That's what you thought all along. Soon, your insurance company sends you a notice that it has generously paid the doctor and the laboratory for the tests and you owe $650 in deductibles.

Being only a layperson, you remain puzzled about what it was that Preventive Medicine prevented. But heck, you can't complain. There's a Health Care Crisis on.

New Roles for Doctors

The number one medical journal in England printed an article recently advocating that medical students be given acting lessons so they can convey better messages of concern and encouragement to patients and their families.

At about the same time, the number one medical journal in the United States published a study showing that surgeons do a better job if there is background music playing in the operating room.

These sound like great strides in medicine.

You're flat on your back in one of those appliances that hospitals call beds, with tubes poked into various inconvenient orifices, and a guy comes in to tell you that you have an infarction of the sternocleidomastoid and they're going to have to replace your neck with PVC pipe.

What doctor would you rather hear that from? Alan Alda, or maybe E. G. Marshall? Or some surgeon with a clammy handshake who keeps looking at his Rolex while he gives you the bad news?

And then they roll you down to the slice and dice area and knock you out. Isn't it comforting to know that while you are sleeping, and the surgeon is making large holes in you and rearranging your insides, he is enjoying records by his favorite singers, like the Rolling Stones or Leon Redbone or House of Pain or Megadeth.

If the acting lessons catch on, and the surgeons who now carve us up a cappella decide to require accompaniment, the medical industry's next step is obvious. There will be two new specialties: Medical Thespian and Surgical Musicologist.

Before the operation, the Surgical Musicologist will come in to ask for your musical preferences, and will compile a list of appropriate Tunes To Be Incised By.

Afterward, the surgeon himself will not have to drop by your room to mention that he isn't sure where he left his favorite little hemostat that his grandmother gave him, but it might be around your duodenum somewhere. The Medical Thespian will substitute, delivering the information in well-measured and eloquent sentences.

These new specialties are sure to happen. One of the major activities of the medical trade is the creation of new specialties. This allows more and more practitioners to wander into your hospital room for four minutes, ask how you're doing and poke the area most likely to hurt.

Such intrusions are known among the gang down at the medical society as "consults." A consult serves two purposes in the healing arts.

One purpose is to contribute to the series of annoyances vital to a hospital patient's well-being. Consults are carefully timed to take place while you are asleep, on the bed pan, being visited by your Aunt Mildred or trying to decide whether the main item on your food tray is an underdone hot dog or an overdone carrot.

The other purpose is to allow physicians whose specialty seems to have no bearing on your medical condition to submit large bills to your health insurance provider.

As these new specialties become more accepted and complex, there may arise a combined Surgical Musicothespian, who will stand in a corner of the operating room and sing show tunes while the less talented doctors work.

Second-Hand Health Hazards

Several humorists have observed that it has become easier to locate the entrances to office buildings in the past year or two; bunches of people are standing just outside the doorways, smoking cigarettes.

This is because a number of building managers and corporate executives have heeded the warnings of the health experts that what is now called second-hand smoke can destroy the lungs of non-smokers who hang out in the same structures as the nicotine addicts.

Our society has concluded that we must do something to stop folks from killing each other by inhaling burning tobacco and then venting the smoke into other people's breathing space. There are legislators who would like to ban public smoking altogether.

It may seem contradictory to crack down on second-hand smoke and not second-hand bullets. But public shooting seems to be protected by the Constitution. So anyone who wants to destroy somebody else's lungs inside most office buildings cannot do it with cigarettes, and will just have to settle for using a pistol, which is quicker but not as subtle.

When you think about the problem of health hazards (a common but discouraging thinking exercise), other things than puffing smoke come to mind that people can do that are hazardous to our health.

They can run over us with an automobile, for instance, and not necessarily a second-hand one.

Okay. I hear you arguing that there is no comparison, because driving is a necessity and smoking is not.

Tell that to most smokers. They'll say that it would be easier to swear off driving than smoking.

So we have gone part way in an attempt to stop other people from creaming us with automobiles by suggesting strongly that they should not drive while drunk. Maybe the first-hand smokers who stand in little hazy clots outside office buildings would prefer a ban on drunken smoking.

Another health hazard: some university researchers recently announced the discovery that women who work in beauty parlors have more miscarriages than those who don't.

The problem is blamed on chemicals used in those establishments, which are apparently very potent. It must take industrial-strength substances to do an acceptable job of beautifying some women.

This leads to the possibility that women will be forced to get their perms and dye jobs on the sidewalk outside the beauty shops, so people inside won't be exposed to second-hand beautification.

The perception of a health hazard can be very subjective. My mother suffered a slight stroke while bending over. Ever since that episode, she says she never bends over.

I have pointed out that it's a good thing she didn't have the stroke while sitting, or she would never sit down. She, in turn, has pointed out that I am a wise-acre kid and she doesn't know where I get it from.

But I'm afraid some university researchers will hear about her bending-over theory, get a grant, do a study, and announce that over-bending is a health hazard, possibly including second-hand bending. Next thing, office building managers will make occupants go outside when they want to bend over.

The Hippo Beat

The problem of missing hippopotami has not been covered thoroughly by any other journalist, which I'm sure endears me to the six persons nationwide who are interested in the subject.

Where's Pablo's Hippopotamus?

Has anybody heard whether the Colombian cops have found Pablo Escobar's hippopotamus?

There were news reports a while back that it was missing. But if there were any later dispatches on the subject, I missed them.

Pablo Escobar was usually described as the drug kingpin of Colombia, before the police there shot him dead, a procedure for handling drug kingpins that has wide approval among civilized persons the world over, when they are not speaking for publication.

The late Senor Escobar earned a lot of money by selling brain-scrambling substances.

He used his profits to buy many things, including a large estate. Being a man of tender heart, he wanted to have some pets on his estate. So he went down to the pet shop and brought home some lions, tigers giraffes, and similarly cuddly animals.

Among the beasts frolicking in the Escobar back yard were three hippopotami. Or, if you prefer, hippopotamuses. The dictionary accepts both. So did Senor Escobar.

Three months after the Colombian government expressed its disapproval of Senor Escobar's activities by filling him with large bullet holes, one of the hippopotamice was reported to have ambled off. It was wandering the countryside, annoying local residents who were not accustomed to seeing a hippopotamus taking up their parking spaces, lolling on their patios or hogging the sidewalk down at the bus stop.

It was not clear why the hippo is suffering from a dose of wanderlust. One account says that the subject of the hippo-hunt is a hippopotamister, and he stomped away in a lovelorn snit after losing a fight with the other hippopotamale over the affections of the third Escobar hippo, who is a hippopotamiss.

That sounds feasible. Or he could be upset over the demise of his owner. Hippopotami don't look sentimental, but you never can tell what deep emotions are lurking inside your average hippopotamus.

The police have tried to track down the half-ton animal. Its former keeper at the estate said he would like to capture it by using drug darts, which would probably please Senor Escobar.

It is somewhat foreign to our thinking here in America del Norte that a hippopotamus would be purchased by a drug kingpin (or queenpin, or princepin, or dukepin, or even an ordinary commonerpin.)

Drug profiteers in these parts usually spend their profits on large four-wheel drive vehicles, gaudy designer jackets, gold chains to drape on their necks and elaborate automatic weapons to use for discouraging the competition.

While I am not totally in touch with the situation, to the best of my knowledge no local drug dealer has yet acquired a hippopotamus, or any other oversized exotic creature.

And a good thing, too. Drug dealers have caused enough problems in inner city neighborhoods.

All that the decent citizens of those areas need to add to their difficulties is a stray hippopotamus lounging in street-corner puddles or coming up to the front porch and begging for a ton of hay.

Having guys walking pit bulls in the neighborhood is bad enough.

The Latest Hippo News

Regular readers of this department who are concerned about hippopotamus activities may be assured that I am keeping an eye on things, while less hippo-oriented news sources tend to offer skimpy hippo coverage.

The hippopotamus aficionados among you will recall that a few weeks ago, I reported that a hippopotamus belonging to Pablo Escobar, the late Colombian drug lord, was missing.

No further word about the hippo's missingness has crossed this desk, which may be the result of indifference to the subject on the part of news gathering organizations.

But I was naturally excited when information arrived from Wisconsin that a hippopotamus had been shot dead in a river there.

Could this be Senor Escobar's wandering hippopotamus? If so, it would probably set a new distance record for hipponauts. The chart in the auto club guide doesn't list the distance from Colombia to Wisconsin, but I'm told it's a long walk.

Don't get excited over the prospect, hippophiles. Investigation reveals that the recently shot hippopotamus was living in a game farm in Wisconsin, got out of its enclosure, waddled five miles and immersed itself cozily in the Mecan River.

The owner of the game farm tracked the beast to the river. He couldn't persuade it to wade out, so he shot it.

Sketchy reports from Wisconsin journalists, who are not often called upon to cover hippopotamus news, do not explain several things. Why was a hippopotamus roaming on a game farm in Wisconsin? Is there a hippo hunting season out there? Did someone mistake it for an elk?

Also, how did the game farmer try to remove the hippo from the river? Shooting it terminally seems a rather drastic and wasteful procedure, so we can assume that he tried every known and available hippo-coaxing method.

Did he call it by name? Tickle it under one or two of its chins? Offer it tempting food? If so, what do hippos consider delicacies?

Is there a hippo of the opposite sex in the vicinity that might have lured the submerged hippo onto the land? If there is another hippo in east-central Wisconsin, can your average Wisconsinite, even a game farmer, identify exactly which sex is its opposite, without getting into a delicate and possibly dangerous situation?

I do understand why the game farmer looked in the river for his hippopotamus. If I were looking for my hippopotamus (I don't have one; this is hippothetical) I would check the nearest river first.

That's because the critter's name is made of words stolen from the Greeks by unprincipled scientists too lazy to name animals decently in English. Hippo means horse, and potamus means river. (I guess potami means two rivers.)

So a hippopotamus is a river horse, and if you are ever so foolish as to acquire your own hippopotamus, and it wanders away as the ones in Colombia and Wisconsin enjoy doing, examine the nearest river first.

The Colombian authorities certainly must have known to inspect rivers, so we can only suppose that the hippopotamus down there remains unswervingly missing.

Watch this space for any further developments.

Moon Coins From Bikini Land

From the vastness of the Pacific Ocean came a sales pitch to buy a souvenir of the Apollo 11 anniversary. It seemed unlikely, but then, you can't expect too much from vastness.

On Top of the Moon Walk

The 25th anniversary of the first human beings strolling around on the moon may have slipped your mind, but in the Marshall Islands they're right on top of it.

A letter came from the Republic of the Marshall Islands Coin Fulfillment Center, offering to honor me by letting me buy a five dollar commemorative coin.

The front of the coin shows astronauts standing on the moon with a flag. On the back is a design that I suspect may be the official seal of the Marshall Islands.

Inscribed below the seal are the words "Jepipilin Ke Ejukaan." Unfortunately, my high school was temporarily not offering Marshallese in the language curriculum on the day I had to choose my courses, so I have no idea what, if anything, "Jepipilin Ke Ejukaan" means. A possible translation is "This coin and $2.95 will get you a Big Mac at the McDonald's in downtown Majuro."

The letter boasts that the Marshall Islanders are willing to sell me their $5 coin for its face value (plus a buck and a half for shipping, handling and insurance.)

It's my firm feeling that if I invest in one of these coins and bequeath it to my grandchildren, someday it may be worth $5, give or take.

The letter assures me that the coin is legal tender. That's encouraging. I wouldn't want to be stuck on some Marshall Island and find out that a cab driver wouldn't take my First Men on the Moon coin for fare.

The coin is, the letter emphasizes, "about the same size as a U.S. silver dollar, yet even thicker." That would sound pretty good, except that elsewhere in the mailing, a small brochure mentions that the coin "is painstakingly minted from gleaming, solid cupronickel." No matter how thick you slice it, that isn't silver.

Curiously, the Marshall Islands Coin Fulfillment Center's return address is in Cheyenne, Wyoming. That area is a bit short on coral atolls, but if it wants to be part of the Marshalls, it's fine with me.

Last I heard, the Marshall Islands are still in the South Pacific. They are a group of 34 reasonable-sized islands and about 1,150 little wannabe islands, a couple of thousand miles southwest of Hawaii. Most of them are coral atolls. Coral is hard stuff some kind of shellfishes build when the mood strikes them.

An atoll is a circle of coral that surrounds a lagoon. A lagoon is a seawater lake.

The Marshalls are in two parallel chains of islands 650 miles long and 130 miles apart. The whole works has only about 70 square miles you can call dry land. If you don't think it sounds much like your neighborhood, you're right.

A British sea captain named John Marshall came upon the islands in 1788, much to his surprise and also the inhabitants.

The local folks, like all good residents of Pacific islands in those days, whiled away their tropical hours raising breadfruit trees and children and lolling in the sun with few clothes on. This sort of behavior has always infuriated persons of European persuasion, so they were told to stop immediately.

After the Marshall Islanders were informed that they were

Marshall Islanders, and not whatever they formerly thought they were, Germany decided the islands belonged to them for a while. Later, when the Germans were busy recovering from those festivities known as World War I, the Japanese decided that it was their turn to own the Marshalls.

In 1944, after the Japanese had bombed Pearl Harbor and otherwise irritated the United States, our armed forces landed on two Marshall islands, Kwajalein, which has the world's largest atoll lagoon, and Eniwetok, also no slouch when it comes to lagooning. Our troops requested that the Japanese deMarshallize themselves. They grudgingly complied.

The United States then did the Marshall Islands the favor of testing nuclear weapons on them. The first hydrogen bomb was exploded on Eniwetok, after that favored isle had already enjoyed seven regular old-fashioned uranium bombs.

Other nuclear explosives were tested on a Marshall atoll named Bikini, which inspired some easily-inspired person to name sexy two-piece bathing suits bikinis. (The Germans had called Bikini atoll Escholtz Island. But for the grace of the fashion gods, sexy two-piece bathing suits might be called escholtzes.)

The government scientists considerately kept moving Marshall Islanders out of their homes and off their atolls, so none of them would be disturbed when their communities were pulverized. Our thoughtful nukers always said they were sorry if anything became radioactive, like all the fish in a lagoon or the mayor's grandmother.

The Marshall Islanders were patient until we got all that atomic bombing out of our systems, and they declared their bunch of islands an independent republic in 1991. There is a big NASA spacecraft tracking station there, which is why the Marshall folks are so interested in moon landings and things.

But I passed on the opportunity to acquire one of their First Men on the Moon five dollar coins. I'm too emotionally attached to the paper kind with Abe Lincoln on it.

Those Nasty Planets

Millions of people believe in astrology, and I don't mean to make fun of them here. (Actually I do, but if you tell them, I'll deny it.) These columns were written in spring and fall of 1993; between those seasons, some planets made the astrologers look good.

The Planets are Acting Up Again

In case your neighborhood astrologer hasn't gotten around to warning you, 1993 is expected to be a heck of a year.

The astrologers, those folks who insist that our faults are not in ourselves but in the stars, report that there is going to be a triple conjunction of the planets Uranus and Neptune this year. And when those two admired and respected planets line up three times in a year, say the stargazers, great events eventualize and great emergencies emerge.

Uranus and Neptune are scheduled to conjunct themselves on February 2, August 20 and October 24.

We have already indulged in a February 2 this year, as you may have noticed, without the Earth's foundations being shaken any more than on most days lately.

But have faith. Have patience. Articles in astrological trade journals assure us that by the time that third conjunction gets conjuncted, the mystic forces of the cosmos will definitely give us what for.

There was, after all, a longitudinal conjunction of Saturn, Uranus and Neptune in the House of Capricorn in 1991, and that signaled the collapse of the Soviet Union, say the astrology buffs.

There seems to be no reason to argue with that, except that the Soviet collapse had been creeping up for several years before 1991 and that the astrologers didn't point out that the longitudinal conjunction predicted the collapse until after the collapse happened.

Those few of use who don't understand what it means to have a longitudinal conjunction of Saturn, Uranus and Neptune in the House of Capricorn are hardly in a position to contradict such potent predictions, even ones made safely after the fact.

And now comes the big 1993 triple conjunction, non-longitudinal and with Saturn not cooperating but again in Capricorn and loaded all the way up to here with astrological portent.

The last three years this happened were 1479, 1650 and 1821.

It takes only a fleeting glance at an encyclopedia to checkup on the astrologers and learn what momentous years the world endures when Uranus and Neptune get triple conjunctivitis.

In 1479, the Turks made peace with the Venetians after 16 years, Ivan the Great made peace with the Tatars, the Bohemians made peace with the Hungarians, Lorenzo the Magnificent made peace with Ferrante of Naples and Leonardo da Vinci invented the parachute. We all know how meaningful those events are to each of our lives.

Under the obvious influence of those clever celestial conjuncters, in 1650 Bishop James Ussher discovered that the world was created in 4004 B.C., Harvard College was chartered and agriculturist Sir Richard Weston advocated the deliberate cultivation of turnips. You can just feel the supernatural tension building as history advances relentlessly toward 1821.

And in that wonderful year, Napoleon died, Dostoevsky was born and Egyptian hieroglyphics were first deciphered. Astrological excitement was unbounded.

Now various astrology publications are promising similarly exhilarating changes in the world for 1993. One writer said there will be natural disasters, scientific breakthroughs, surprising corporate mergers and government scandals.

That sounds curiously like years when we don't have any triple planetary conjunctions, too.

Are the Planets Clobbering Us?

Last March this column reported that astrologers had declared 1993 to be a year of turmoil and calamity.

The professional journals of the stargazing industry, ever alert for shenanigans in the heavens, noticed that 1993 was scheduled to endure a triple conjunction of the planets Uranus and Neptune. And when those two well-known and influential planets line up three times in a year, all sorts of excitement is inflicted on the human race.

Astrology publications promised that if we all paid attention, we would see assorted natural disasters, scientific breakthroughs, surprising corporate mergers and government scandals.

I confess that my previous report on the subject treated it with some skepticism.

But the way 1993 has been proceeding, I may have to apologize to the astrologators, if not to the planets involved.

Uranus and Neptune neatly conjuncted themselves as advertised, on February 2 and August 20. The third conjuncterization is due on October 24, and there is little reason to think they won't up and conjunct again. Planets are nothing if not reliable.

And since spring, when I fired that salvo of low-caliber derision at the astrological import of this odd celestial behavior, look at what's been happening.

We've enjoyed the Blizzard of '93. We had a record-breaking heat wave. Parts of the country have had a drought. The midwest got the Mississippi River all over it. A whole Amtrak train fell in a swamp. India got earthquaked.

The Japanese government changed parties for the first time since Douglas MacArthur decided to let them alone. The Palestinians and the Israelis shook hands. The Russian Revolution tried to make a comeback.

Mattel toy company bought Fisher-Price toys. AT&T bought McCaw, the biggest cable TV operation. Something mergerish is happening to Paramount. Volvo merged with Daimler.

Julia Roberts married Lyle Lovett.

Randall Cunningham snapped a fibula. The Phillies won the pennant.

All of this unlikeliness socked us with only two of the three conjunctions completed. The third one is almost upon us, and after that the year still has a couple of months for more startling happenings to happen.

At this stage of planetary influence, I wouldn't be surprised if Madonna became a nun; if Congress passed Clinton's health care plan unanimously without debate; if John Kruk got slim; if the KKK integrated; if the missing Mars probe came home by itself; if Lloyd Bentsen announced that he spotted an error in the books, and there isn't any federal deficit after all; if Rush Limbaugh is exposed as a former KGB agent; if General Cinema, General Dynamics, General Electric, General Mills and General Motors all merged and formed the General Most Everything Corporation.

Who knows what the planets might pull off next?

Let's hope that Uranus and Neptune don't have it in for me because of last spring's flippancy. I look up at the sky apprehensively when I go out the door, worrying that those planets might have noticed what I wrote about them, got ticked off and decided to conjunct me some night when I'm not expecting it.

And to All, a Good Night

These items should be read in about mid-December, just before donning your gay apparel and calling in the hall-deckers.

A Dickens of a Cowboy Yarn

There warn't a mite of doubt that Jake Marley died with his boots on.

The M was still in the brand of the S-Bar-M Ranch, but Big Eb Scrooge was in the saddle, and he was riding alone, pardners. And Big Eb was the orneriest, no-goodest, low-down sidewindin' polecat in these parts, and that includes greasers and most injuns.

Why, when his own nephew trotted his pinto up to the ranch house to wish Big Eb a merry Christmas, the old coot come out on the porch with a shotgun and says, "Humbug, dagnab it! Git off my property fore I runs you off!"

And I wouldn't treat a rattlesnake the way Big Eb treated his top hand, Slim Cratchit.

"Please, Big Eb, suh," says Slim, "cain't I wait until the day after Christmas afore I goes off on that 2,000 mile cattle drive you got scheduled to start December 25?"

"Cuss it, man," snarls Big Eb, "next thing you'll be asking me to let you use a horse."

"But I want to be home with my young-un, Tiny Tex," Slim pleads. "He's been feeling poorly ever since that coyote chawed his laig off."

"Well, okay," says Big Eb, reluctant-like, "but I expect you to work 366 days next year to make up for it."

Well, sir, Big Eb gobbles down some hard tack and beans and turns in for the night. Quicker'n a woke-up jackrabbit, up pops the late Jake Marley alongside Eb's bunk, dragging his saddle and tack and branding irons and such.

"Hellfire and damnation!" cusses old Eb.

"That's about the size of it, pilgrim," says Jake's ghost, "less'n you start in riding tall and shooting straight. Now, three ghosts I been bunking with are gonna sashay in here and set you to a-heading proper down the Yuletide trail."

"I think I druther wrassle a cactus," moans Big Eb, shaking like a heifer in a bullpen. But it were too late. In lopes the Ghost of Old-Timey Christmas.

This ghost gets Big Eb recollecting how Christmas Day was before he got himself all meaned up; how he used to ride into town wearing his shirt with the mother of pearl buttons, show off with his Winchester at the turkey shoot, give out silver dollars to his friends and acquaintances and dance all night with the prettiest gals at the shivaree down at the church hall.

Next thing, along rambles the Ghost of Christmas Nowadays. This spook shows Big Eb what a nasty cuss he's been acting like, what with Eb's nephew allowing that it would be less painful to set down on his spurs than to have an uncle like Eb, and little Tiny Tex pitifully cheering up his dad by saying that his leg problem would at least help the family save money on stirrups.

Lastly comes the Ghost of Newfangled Christmas, who convinces Big Eb that if he don't mend his harness, he's in for an early trip to boot hill and won't nobody care two hoots down the rain barrel that he's gone to his last roundup.

Well, pardners, I'll be willow-switched if Big Eb didn't change direction faster than a longhorn herd that come on a rattler. He rode out and shot a couple of fat range hens for Christmas dinners for his nephew and for Slim Cratchit. He give Slim a cayuse to use around the spread, and carved a fancy crutch for Tiny Tex outen an old broke buckboard shaft, to which the little nipper ups and says, "God bless the whole dang bunch of us".

And these here days, folks down thataway say that nary a soul has a more rip-roaring, sod-busting, gullywasher of a good time at Christmas than Big Eb Scrooge.

A Modern Child's Query

Dear Editor Dude:

Some of my little buds around the hood tell me that Santa Claus is an outdated white European male, and is no longer politically correct. This has me totally amped, because I am afraid he won't bring me any new Nintendo games, which cost some extremely rad fundage if I have to save for them out of my completely weak allowance.

My daddy says there is no use asking a journalism dude, because you can't believe anything you read in the papers, but I thought I would give it a shot anyhow. Give me the straight stuff, man: Should I believe in this old dude with the white beard, or what?

> Chill out,
> Kimberly.

Dear Kim:

Yes, Kimberly, Santa Claus is truly excellent.

Not believe in him? Why, you might as well not believe in D. B. Cooper or Ninja Turtles or Wilt Chamberlin's sex life. You might as well not believe that the government is covering up visits by space aliens or that Elvis is working nights at a 7-Eleven in Omaha.

If there were no Santa Claus, what would happen to Toys R Us or Hallmark?

Whose lap would little kids sit on to have their pictures taken squirming and crying, so their parents can have fuzzy and faded color photos to save for 13 years and embarrass them by showing the picture to their first serious sweethearts?

What would happen to all the cheap red suits and black plastic belts and mangy synthetic beards and wigs hidden in the back of the top shelf of closets all over the civilized world? What would high school bands do on Thanksgiving Day with no fat old dude to escort to some department store?

Would anybody so much as watch out or not cry, if nobody is coming to town?

Kimberly, your buds in the hood are wrong. Their wrongness is major to the max. They have been bummed out by the skepticism of a skeptical age. They do not believe unless they see it on the Nightly News With Tom Brokaw.

They have seen Milli Vanilli caught being dubbed, and Michael Jackson buying noses by the case, and Shannen duking it out with other babes in bars, and they are so fully edged and basically freaked that they cannot get it into their skanky melons that anything is rad and fresh unless they can cruise around in it, mack out on it, dance to it or otherwise party with it. Even old dudes acquire this kind of totally burnt attitude. It's sad.

No Santa Claus? That's way bogus. He lives, and hangs out forever. A thousand years from now, Kimberly, nay, 10,000 years from now, he will continue to make awesome the heart of childhood.

Kim, you aren't related to some old babe named Virginia, are you?

Well, as Santa Claus is fond of saying, "Merry Christmas to all, and party on."

A Call to the North Pole

This year I decided to call Santa Claus at his 800 number.

Last year, the traditional letter didn't get to him in time. The Post Office returned it because it didn't have the nine-digit zip code for the North Pole.

Then it got misdelivered to North Paola, Kansas, and by the time it was forwarded it was Dec. 28 and I never did get what I asked for: a copy of the 1993 John Kruk Etiquette Guide, a fruit cake saw, a set of MacNeil Lehrer NewsHour action figures, a Save the Bumpers sticker to put on my whale, a Hooked on Quantum Physics course and an Official NFL Blow Out Your Knees on Astroturf board game.

So I tried Santa's toll free number. It's 1-800-BLI-TZEN.

The phone rang a few times, and then a recorded voice said: "Merry Christmas. Thank you for calling the Santa Claus North Pole hotline. If you are submitting your Christmas list, press one. If you are complaining about last year's delivery, press two. If you are trying to reach a specific elf or reindeer and know the extension, you may enter it now. Otherwise, press three. If you are annoyed by this kind of stupid electronic telephone system, press four. Thank you."

I pressed one.

There were a few rings. Then a cheery voice recited: "All of our elves are busy. Your call will be taken by the next available elf."

The phone began emitting a recording of "March of the Wooden Soldiers" played by the Kiwanis Philharmonic of Mulespit, Missouri.

A voice interrupted at one point: "I'm sorry, our elves are still busy handling requests from greedy little callers just like you. Please stay on the line, and remember, we recommend watching out, and it's preferable not to cry or pout..."

At that point, there was another ring, and a voice said, "Santa's Workshop. How may I help you?"

"I have my Christmas list here..."

"May I have your account number?" the voice interrupted.

"I'm sorry," I stammered. "I don't have an account number."

"Well, under our new computerized, microchipped, automated hi-tech Christmas list fulfillment system, you'll need an account number for guaranteed Christmas Eve delivery. I'll just need a little information:

"Name? Date of birth? Sex? Street address? City? State? Zip code? Social Security number?

"Chimney size? Is that connected to a working fireplace? Stocking size? Will you be supplying a pre-ornamented tree, or do we trim? What is your estimated Christmas Eve bedtime? Is anyone in the household allergic to reindeer fur?

"Thank you for the information. You'll be getting your plastic card and a complete gift recipient's information kit in a few days."

"Christmas will be over by then," I protested.

"We make allowances for that. Just let me get you up on the screen here and check your status."

I heard some keys clicking.

"Sir," the elf said placidly, "Santa has made his list, and I've checked it twice. I find you in column one, Naughty, and I'm afraid you don't appear in column two, Nice. But maybe next year. Merry Christmas."

The Origin of Some Christmas Customs

Every December, stories are written about the origin of Christmas traditions.

Writers tell how the custom of hanging wreaths began, who hung the first stockings by a fireplace, why we decorate evergreen trees and who wrote the Christmas carols.

But many things people do at Christmas time have never been traced back to their beginnings. Here is the result of some depth research into Yuletide history: the origin of several well-known Christmas customs.

Getting a Tree Too Tall for the Living Room:
This custom, practiced in many homes, was started by Hans Grosserbaum, a German, about 1580.

Grosserbaum, the legend says, insisted that the tree would fit, and bought it over his wife's objections.

When he got the tree home and it wouldn't stand upright without scraping the ceiling, Grosserbaum's wife began saying that she had told him so, and that he was a dumbhead, etc.

He left his wife holding the tree and went to get his axe. Old accounts vary as to what he did then.

The Unassembled Bicycle:
The bicycle that arrives on Christmas Eve in 127 pieces and has to be put together by a mechanically inept father was the creation of two brothers, Orville and Wilbur Tantrum, who were unsuccessful airplane manufacturers.

They hit on the idea after a triplane that wouldn't get off the ground ran over a neighbor's velocipede and smashed it to bits.

Their first successful Unassembled Bicycle was delivered to Charles J. Doppelfinger on Christmas Eve, 1908. While the Tantrum Brothers stood proudly watching, Doppelfinger worked for an hour without being able to put the bike together. Finally, he threw a Tantrum down the front steps.

The brothers made later improvements to the Unassembled Bicycle by creating the Unintelligible Instruction Sheet to go with it, and in 1911, perfected it when they conceived the idea of omitting one small but essential bolt.

Throwing Out the $5 Bill
from Aunt Emma With the Wrappings:

This is a peculiarly American contribution to Christmas tradition, and it is observed, with variations, in hundreds of homes.

The initiator of this quaint custom is said to have been Martha Louise Crumple, of Sawbuck, W. Va.

It was Christmas night of 1886 that Miss Crumple, then 12 years old, realized that the $5 bill sent to her by her Aunt Emma had vanished. Frantic and tearful searching of the waste can in the coal bin finally turned up the greenback, squashed in with the poinsettia-printed tissue paper that had been wrapped around the cast-iron apple corer from Cousin Winesap.

The Breaking of the Toys:

Time has hidden the name of the first child who succeeded in wrecking all the new toys by sundown on Christmas Day.

But who is not acquainted with the sound of gleeful laughter around the Christmas tree as the children take part in this holiday ritual?

And who is not familiar with the sharp smack of parental palm on childish epidermis that is the traditional ending to this Yuletide activity?

Nothing Like a Good Book

We have arrived, gentle reader, at the end of this accumulation of slightly-used newspaper columns. It seems fitting to conclude with a column that contained information from an actual publisher about how to recognize a good book.

The Best Book Possible

It was pleasant to know that the book I was going to read was a good book. There is nothing I like better than a good book, except most of my relatives and friends and possibly meat loaf. A blurb on the back of the book assured me that it was a good one.

It blurbed as follows:

"We have made every effort to make this the best book possible. Our paper is opaque, with minimal show-through; it will not discolor or become brittle with age. Pages are sewn in signatures, in the method traditionally used for the best books, and will not drop out, as often happens with paperbacks held together with glue. Books open flat for easy reference. The binding will not crack or split. This is a permanent book."

Wow. What a book.

The back of the book said a few nice things about the author, too. But it wasn't nearly as enthusiastic about him, and the stuff he wrote that was presumably printed therein, as it was about every effort that made it the best book possible.

This is a publisher who knows what is important to us book-loving persons.

That opaque paper is a great idea. Who wants to be reading the next page, backward, through the page you actually want to be reading? Transparent pages would keep giving away plot surprises.

I checked inside the book, and the publisher was right. I had to hold pages up to the light if I wanted to see through them. Which I didn't.

Also, no pages dropped out. At least, not while I was looking. And you wouldn't want that to happen, except maybe from "War and Peace" or Will Durant's "The Story of Civilization," where a couple of pages falling out here and there would never be missed.

I tried to open the book flat for easy reference. It immediately closed itself up again with a lazy but determined motion. But that was all right. It was a book of old Robert Benchley articles from "Liberty Magazine" in the early 1930s, and not likely to be used for reference. At least, not around our house.

And as I watched, the final promise was kept. The binding neither cracked nor split.

The blurb didn't even mention that the book has a nice bright blue cover.

But it is edifying to know that I own a good book. I've been leaving it lying around the house, hoping that kids in the family will come upon it and learn to appreciate good books, too.

Then, someday when they are grown up and able to appreciate such things, they will come to me carrying a copy of a book by William Faulkner or Charles Dickens or Fannie Hurst, and say, "I'm reading a really good book. It has opaque pages sewn in signatures, and it opens flat for easy reference. It has a whole bunch of words in it, too. I think maybe they're literature or something."

Additional copies of
"Soggy Shrub Rides Again and other improbabilities",
may be ordered from your bookstore, (the order number is
ISBN 0-9603924-9-1), or by sending $16.95, per copy,
which includes shipping & handling to:

Enoch Flower Publishing
P. O. Box 27666P
Philadelphia PA 19118

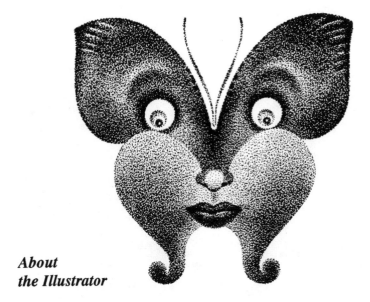

About the Illustrator

Bea Weidner is a professional illustrator with (what seems like) several lifetimes in the graphic arts field.

Her brilliant work has appeared in books for Anchor Press/Doubleday, Silver Burdette & Ginn, Instructo, McGraw Hill and Macmillan & Co.; in such magazines as *The Atlantic Monthly, the Magazine of the American Enterprise Institute, Nursing, Learning* and *Ranger Rick's* (The National Wildlife Federation); and in the editorial pages of the *Philadelphia Inquirer* and *Inside Magazine.*

She is also a published author, writing articles for *Greenscene*, the magazine of the Pennsylvania Horticultural Society.

Bea Weidner has taught illustration at Moore College of Art and The University of the Arts., her alma mater.

Her work has hung in shows at the Society of Illustrators in New York and has been published in that society's annuals and those of *Graphis*. She has enjoyed various accolades from the Art Directors Clubs of New York and Philadelphia.

Her most recent outburst of creativity is baking edible pictures – 3-D dough art – a very tasty approach to illustration.

About the Author:

James Smart's column appears in weekly newspapers published by Intercounty Newspaper Group in the Philadelphia area. Readers have been familiar with his work in local publications for 45 years, and have not yet run him out of town.

He was a staff member of the old *Philadelphia Bulletin* for 25 years, including 14 years as a columnist. He later contributed regularly to *The Bulletin* until it closed in 1982, meanwhile committing such other career peccadillos as being vice president of a public relations agency, editor of two local business publications, and media relations manager for a large bank.

But he finally was able to resist the siren lure of adequate remuneration, and returned to column writing. Once more he can bask in the glow of venomous disapproval in letters from readers who take him too seriously.

Smart lives in the Mount Airy section of Philadelphia with his wife, Barbara Torode, a graphic designer.